EPHESIANS:
Grace Changes Everything

ROBERT GRIFFITH

Copyright © 2025 Grace and Truth Publishing

All rights reserved. No part of this book may be reproduced, stored in a retrieval system, or transmitted in any form, without the written permission of Grace and Truth Publishing.

GRACE AND TRUTH PUBLISHING
PO Box 338, Gunnedah NSW 2380 Australia
www.graceandtruthpublishing.com.au

All Bible quotes are from the New International Version (NIV) expect where otherwise stated.

NEW INTERNATIONAL VERSION (NIV), Copyright 1973, 1978 and 1984 by international Bible Society. Used by permission of Zondervan Publishing House. All rights reserved.

Other version quotes are from:

AMPLIFIED BIBLE (AMP), Copyright © 1954, 1958, 1962, 1964, 1965, 1987 by The Lockman Foundation. Used by permission.

ENGLISH STANDARD VERSION (ESV), Copyright © 2001 by Crossway Bibles, a division of Good News Publishers. Used by permission. All rights reserved.

NEW AMERICAN STANDARD BIBLE (NASB), Copyright © 1960, 1962, 1963, 1968, 1971, 1972, 1973, 1975, 1977, by The Lockman Foundation. Used by permission.

NEW KING JAMES VERSION (NKJV), Copyright © 1979, 1980, 1982, by Thomas Nelson Inc. Used by permission. All rights reserved.

THE MESSAGE (MSG), by Eugene Peterson, Copyright © 1993, 1994, 1995, 1996, and 2000. Used by permission of NavPress Publishing Group. All rights reserved.

REVISED STANDARD VERSION (RSV), Copyright © 1973, by Thomas Nelson Inc. Used by permission. All rights reserved.

Quotes in square brackets are the author's comment.

ISBN 978-1-7635504-2-1

TABLE OF CONTENTS

1. Introduction 4
2. The Riches of God's Grace 13
3. Prayer for Spiritual Wisdom 23
4. Alive in Christ 33
5. Unity in Christ 43
6. The Mystery Revealed 54
7. Paul's Prayer 66
8. Worthy of our Calling 75
9. Old Self, New Self 85
10. Children of Light 95
11. Housekeeping 107
12. The Armour of God 118
13. Final Exhortations 129

1. INTRODUCTION

The book of Ephesians really stands out as one of the most theologically rich and practical New Testament letters. This letter serves not only as a guide to the Ephesian believers but also as a timeless message for the entire church, both then and now. It is a call to both recognize and embrace the overwhelming grace and spiritual blessings we have been given in Christ, and to live in a manner that reflects these truths in every aspect of our lives.

Throughout this study we will be exploring the depths of teaching in this incredible letter, not merely for intellectual understanding, but especially for life transformation. In this introductory chapter, I want to provide an overview of the book, hopefully helping us to frame our journey ahead by understanding the full context, purpose, themes, and the practical applications of this remarkable epistle.

The author and recipients

The letter to the Ephesians is traditionally attributed to the Apostle Paul, as indicated in the opening verse: *"Paul, an apostle of Christ Jesus by the will of God."* (1:1) Paul wrote this letter during his imprisonment in Rome, which is why it is known as one of the 'Prison Epistles' with Philippians, Colossians and Philemon.

The recipients of this letter are described as *"God's holy people in Ephesus, the faithful in Christ Jesus"* (1:1). While the letter is addressed to the church in Ephesus, some early manuscripts omit the phrase *"in Ephesus,"* which has led many scholars to conclude that this letter was actually intended to be circulated among the various churches in the whole region.

Ephesus, a major city in Asia Minor, was known for its wealth, trade, and religious diversity. It was home to the Temple of Artemis, one of the Seven Wonders of the Ancient World, which made it a hub for pagan worship. The Ephesian church was established during Paul's third missionary journey (Acts 19), and it flourished in this city despite the challenges of its surrounding culture.

Paul's relationship with the Ephesian church was deep and personal. He spent more than two years ministering there, teaching both Jews and Greeks about the kingdom of God (Acts 19:10). His heart for these believers is evident in his writing, as he desires for them to fully grasp the magnitude of their new identity in Christ and the spiritual riches that come with it.

The purpose of the letter

Unlike some of Paul's other letters, Ephesians does not appear to address specific problems within the church, such as the false teaching dealt with in Galatians or the divisions found in 1 Corinthians. Instead, Ephesians reads more like a general manifesto on Christian living and the nature of the Church. It is a letter that celebrates the unity of believers in Christ and encourages them to live in a manner worthy of their calling. Paul's purpose in this Epistle is fivefold:

1. *Reveal the mystery of the gospel:* Paul emphasizes the mystery that was hidden for ages but is now revealed in Christ. This mystery is that both Jews and Gentiles are united as one body in Christ (3:6).

2. *Remind believers of their spiritual blessings:* Paul begins the letter with a doxology of praise, reminding the Ephesians of the incredible spiritual blessings they have in Christ, such as adoption, redemption, and the sealing of the Holy Spirit (1:3-14).

3. *Encourage unity and love:* A major issue in this letter is unity in the body of Christ. Paul calls for believers to maintain the unity of the Spirit through the bond of peace, recognizing that there is *"one body and one Spirit... one Lord, one faith, one baptism."* (4:4-5)

4. *Call for holy living:* In the second half of the letter, Paul gives practical exhortations, encouraging believers to live out their new identity in Christ. This includes living with integrity, kindness, and love, and rejecting immorality, greed, and deceit (4:17-5:21).

5. *Prepare believers for spiritual warfare:* The letter concludes with a powerful passage on the armour of God, reminding believers how they have already been equipped in Christ to stand firm against the schemes of the devil. (6:10-18)

Five key themes in Ephesians

1. The riches of God's grace

From the very outset, Paul emphasizes the vast riches of God's grace that have been lavished upon believers. In Ephesians 1:3-14, Paul delivers a sweeping summary of the blessings that come from being in Christ, reminding the believers that they have been chosen, redeemed, forgiven, and sealed by the Holy Spirit.

He declares, *"In him we have redemption through his blood, the forgiveness of sins, in accordance with the riches of God's grace that he lavished on us."* (1:7-8) This theme of grace runs throughout the letter. Perhaps most famously, Ephesians 2:8-9 teaches that salvation is by grace through faith: *"For it is by grace you have been saved, through faith - and this is not from yourselves, it is the gift of God - not by works, so that no one can boast."*

For Paul, grace changes everything! The grace of God is not only the basis for our salvation, but it is also the foundation for how we every day. Grace is the empowering presence of God, which enables us to love, forgive and walk in humility and righteousness. This theme will be a central point in each sermon as we unpack the incredible generosity of God's grace towards us.

2. The unity of the Church

Unity in the body of Christ is also a dominant theme in Ephesians. Paul stresses that the dividing wall between Jews and Gentiles has been torn down in Christ, and both groups are now united as one people. He writes, *"His purpose was to create in himself one new humanity out of the two, thus making peace."* (2:15)

This unity is not merely ethnic but also spiritual. Believers are called to be united in faith, hope, and love. Paul's call for unity is grounded in the truth that there is one body, one Spirit, one Lord, one faith, one baptism, and one God and Father of all (4:4-6). This unity is a testament to the reconciling power of the gospel, and Paul urges believers to *"make every effort to keep the unity of the Spirit through the bond of peace."* (4:3)

3. The Church as the body of Christ

Ephesians presents one of the most profound pictures of the Church in the New Testament: The Church as the body of Christ.

Paul writes, *"And God placed all things under his feet and appointed him to be head over everything for the church, which is his body, the fullness of him who fills everything in every way."* (1:22-23)

This metaphor of the Church as the body of Christ carries significant implications for how we view ourselves and our relationship with one another. Each believer is a vital part of the body, and Christ is the head. We are interconnected and dependent on one another, each fulfilling different roles and functions within the body. This idea will be explored further as we consider the gifts that God has given to the Church to equip and build it up (4:11-16).

4. Walking worthy of our calling

Paul spends the first three chapters of Ephesians laying out the theological foundations of the gospel, but in the latter half of the letter, he turns to practical application. In Ephesians 4:1, Paul urges the believers to *"live a life worthy of the calling you have received."* This calling is the high calling of being a follower of Christ, and it demands a life that reflects the character of God.

The call to holy living is not a call to legalism or self-righteousness, but rather a response to the grace we have received. It is a call to put off the old self and submit to the new self, as we are created to be like God in true righteousness and holiness (4:22-24). This transformation affects every area of our lives - our relationships, our speech, our work, and our attitudes and conduct.

In the coming chapters, I will explore what it means to walk in love, light, and wisdom (5:1-21).

5. Spiritual warfare

Ephesians concludes with a vivid and sobering reminder that we are engaged in a spiritual battle. Paul writes, *"For our struggle is not against flesh and blood, but against the rulers, against the authorities, against the powers of this dark world and against the spiritual forces of evil in the heavenly realms."* (6:12)

He then exhorts the believers to *"put on the full armour of God"* so that they can stand firm against the devil's schemes (6:11). The armour which God has given us in Christ: truth, righteousness, the gospel of peace, faith, salvation, the Word of God, and prayer - equips us for this spiritual warfare.

We will unpack this imagery further and deal with some deceptive teaching which has accompanied this passage for many years now.

Application for today

As we embark on this journey through the book of Ephesians, it is crucial to recognize that the themes and truths presented in Ephesians are not merely ancient ideas but are deeply relevant for us today. The church in Ephesus, much like the modern church, lived in a world full of spiritual and cultural challenges.

Yet, Paul's message to them is also God's message to us: we have been richly blessed with every spiritual blessing in Christ, and we are called to live in light of these truths. Here are some ways we can apply the key themes of Ephesians to our lives today.

Embracing our identity in Christ ...

One of the primary messages of Ephesians is the believer's identity in Christ. Paul wants us to understand that we are chosen, adopted, redeemed, and sealed by the Holy Spirit (1:4-14). This identity is not based on our performance but on God's grace. In a world where people often struggle with questions of self-worth and identity, Ephesians reminds us that our true identity is always and only found in Jesus Christ.

We must constantly remind ourselves that we are not defined by our past, our failures, or even our successes. We are defined by what God says about us in Christ. This truth should shape how we view ourselves and how we live out our faith. When we know who we are in Christ, we can walk confidently in the world, knowing that we are deeply loved and secure in Him.

Living in unity ...

In a time when divisions, both inside and outside the church, seem to be at an all-time high, the call for unity in Ephesians is as timely as ever. Whether it's racial, political, or theological divisions, the Church is not immune to the forces that seek to tear apart relationships and communities. Paul's call for unity is grounded in the gospel, which tells us that we have been reconciled to God and to one another (2:14-18).

As the body of Christ, we are called to reflect the unity of the Spirit, even in the midst of diversity. This means pursuing peace, bearing with one another in love, and making every effort to maintain the bond of peace (4:2-3).

In practical terms, unity requires humility, patience, and a commitment to love others as Christ has loved us. It means choosing to forgive when we've been wronged and working toward reconciliation in our relationships. The unity of the Church is a powerful testimony to the world of the reconciling power of the gospel, and it is a theme we will explore throughout this series.

Walking in holiness ...

The call to live a life worthy of our calling (4:1) challenges us to examine our daily conduct and how it aligns with our new identity in Christ.

Holiness is not about following a set of rules or achieving moral perfection; it is about being transformed by the Spirit of God and living in a way that reflects the character of Christ within us.

As we move through Ephesians, we will see that holy living affects every area of our lives - our speech, our actions, our relationships, and even our thoughts. In a culture that often promotes selfishness, greed, and immorality, Paul's words in Ephesians 4:22-24 are a reminder that we are called to put off the old self and be renewed in the attitude of our minds. We are to embrace the new self, created to be like God in true righteousness and holiness.

This transformation is not something we accomplish on our own; it is the work of the Holy Spirit in us. As we seek to walk in holiness, we must rely on the Spirit's power and daily surrender to His leading.

In this book, we will learn how to practically live out our faith in a way that honours God and reflects His holiness to the world around us.

Standing firm in spiritual warfare ...

The reality of spiritual warfare is so often overlooked or misunderstood in the modern church, yet Ephesians 6 reminds us that we are in a battle - not against flesh and blood, but against spiritual forces of evil (6:12). Paul's exhortation to put on the full armour of God is not just a metaphorical concept; it is a practical guide for how we can stand firm in our faith amid spiritual opposition.

In today's world, the enemy's tactics are often subtle, and the pressures of culture, temptation, and fear can easily lead us astray if we are not vigilant.

Paul's instruction to stand firm by daily embracing truth, righteousness, faith, salvation, and the Word of God will be essential in equipping us to live victorious lives in Christ.

As we study the armour of God in the final chapter of this series, I will explore this important metaphor in more detail. The battle is real, but God has already provided everything we need to stand firm. Our victory is not in our strength, but in the power of God working in and through us.

Conclusion

The letter to the Ephesians is a profound invitation for us to explore the riches of God's amazing grace and to live out the implications of our identity in Christ. It offers us a glimpse into the mind of Paul, who is not only a theologian but a pastor at heart, desiring that the church grows in spiritual maturity, unity, and holiness.

As we journey through each chapter of Paul's letter, we will uncover the depths of his teaching and apply it to our lives today. We will learn about the incredible blessings we have in Christ, the power of God's grace, the unity of the Church, the call to holy living, and the reality of spiritual warfare.

As we prepare to dive deeper into this letter, let us be open to the transformative work of the Holy Spirit in our lives. Let us embrace our identity in Christ, pursue unity with one another, walk in holiness, and stand firm in the face of spiritual battles.

Together, we will discover that grace changes everything as the empowering presence of God, in Christ, equips us to live lives which are worthy of the calling we have received.

2. THE RICHES OF GOD'S GRACE

This letter, written by the Apostle Paul, is filled with profound theological insights and practical guidance for our daily Christian walk. In this chapter, I will first examine the opening fourteen verses, where Paul introduces himself, blesses God for the spiritual blessings we have in Christ, and outlines the incredible riches of God's grace.

> **Ephesians 1:1-14** "*Paul, an apostle of Christ Jesus by the will of God, to God's holy people in Ephesus, the faithful in Christ Jesus: Grace and peace to you from God our Father and the Lord Jesus Christ.*
>
> *Praise be to the God and Father of our Lord Jesus Christ, who has blessed us in the heavenly realms with every spiritual blessing in Christ. For he chose us in him before the creation of the world to be holy and blameless in his sight. In love he predestined us for adoption to sonship through Jesus Christ, in accordance with his pleasure and will - to the praise of his glorious grace, which he has freely given us in the One he loves.*
>
> *In him we have redemption through his blood, the forgiveness of sins, in accordance with the riches of God's grace that he lavished on us. With all wisdom and understanding, he made known to us the mystery of his will according to his good pleasure, which he purposed in Christ, to be put into effect when the times reach their fulfillment - to bring unity to all things in heaven and on earth under Christ. In him we were also chosen, having been predestined according to the plan of him who works out everything in conformity with the purpose of his will, in order that we, who were the first to put our hope in Christ, might be for the praise of his glory.*

And you also were included in Christ when you heard the message of truth, the gospel of your salvation. When you believed, you were marked in him with a seal, the promised Holy Spirit, who is a deposit guaranteeing our inheritance until the redemption of those who are God's possession - to the praise of his glory."

This passage is packed with profound truths about who we are in Christ and the incredible blessings we have received through God's grace. We will break down this passage into three main sections: Paul's greeting and blessing (1-3), the spiritual blessings in Christ (4-10), and the assurance of our inheritance (11-14).

Paul's greeting and blessing (1:1-3)

Paul begins his letter with a standard greeting, identifying himself as *"an apostle of Christ Jesus by the will of God."* This introduction establishes his authority and the divine calling behind his message. Paul then addresses his audience as *"God's holy people in Ephesus, the faithful in Christ Jesus."*

Grace and peace ...

Paul extends a blessing of grace and peace from God our Father and the Lord Jesus Christ. These two words, *grace* and *peace*, are central to Paul's message and the Christian life. Grace is God's empowering presence the foundation of our salvation. Peace is the result of this grace, a profound sense of well-being and reconciliation with God.

Spiritual blessings ...

Paul transitions from his greeting to a doxology, praising God for the spiritual blessings we have in Christ. *"Praise be to the God and Father of our Lord Jesus Christ, who has blessed us in the heavenly realms with every spiritual blessing in Christ."*

This verse sets the tone for the rest of the passage as it emphasizes the abundance and the completeness of the blessings we have received.

The spiritual blessings in Christ (1:4-10)

In this section, Paul outlines several key blessings we receive through our relationship with Christ. These blessings are not just material or temporary but are spiritual and eternal, rooted in the heavenly realms.

Chosen in Christ ...

"For he chose us in him before the creation of the world to be holy and blameless in his sight." This profound truth reminds us that our relationship with God is not based on our own efforts but on His sovereign choice. Before the world was created, God chose us to be His own, setting us apart to live holy and blameless lives. Being chosen by God before the creation of the world underscores the eternal nature of His love and purpose for us. It is a humbling and awe-inspiring thought that God knew us and set His affection on us before we even existed. This should fill us with gratitude and a deep sense of security in our identity in Christ.

Predestined for adoption ...

"In love he predestined us for adoption to sonship through Jesus Christ, in accordance with his pleasure and will." Our adoption as God's children is a result of His love and predestined plan. Through Christ, we are brought into God's family, enjoying all the rights and privileges of sonship. This adoption is not based on our merit but on God's grace and His pleasure and will. The concept of adoption is rich with meaning. In the Roman world, adoption was a powerful act that gave the adopted person a new status and inheritance rights.

Similarly, our spiritual adoption means that we have been given a new identity and a share in the inheritance of God's kingdom. We are no longer strangers or outsiders but beloved children of God with all the accompanying rights and responsibilities.

Redemption and forgiveness ...

"In him we have redemption through his blood, the forgiveness of sins, in accordance with the riches of God's grace that he lavished on us." Redemption and forgiveness are central to our salvation. Through the shed blood of Christ, we are redeemed from the bondage of sin and forgiven of all our transgressions. This redemption is a demonstration of the riches of God's grace, which He has generously lavished upon us.

Redemption involves being bought back or set free from slavery. In our case, it means being set free from the slavery of sin and death. The cost of our redemption was the precious blood of Christ, highlighting the immense value God places on us. Forgiveness, which accompanies redemption, means that our sins are no longer held against us. We are cleansed and made new, able to stand before God without guilt or shame.

Revealing the mystery of His will ...

"With all wisdom and understanding, he made known to us the mystery of his will according to his good pleasure, which he purposed in Christ, to be put into effect when the times reach their fulfillment - to bring unity to all things in heaven and on earth under Christ." God, in His wisdom and understanding, has revealed to us the mystery of His will. This mystery is His plan to unite all things in heaven and on earth under Christ. This cosmic plan demonstrates God's ultimate purpose and sovereignty.

The "*mystery*" Paul refers to is not something hidden or unknowable but rather something that was previously hidden and has now been revealed. God's plan to bring everything together under Christ was not fully understood until Christ came and completed His work of redemption.

This plan is truly comprehensive, affecting not only our individual lives but the entire cosmos. It gives us a sense of our place in God's grand design and reassures us that history is moving toward a glorious fulfillment in Christ.

The assurance of our inheritance (1:11-14)

In the final section of this passage, Paul assures us of our inheritance in Christ and the guarantee of the Holy Spirit.

Chosen according to His plan ...

"In him we were also chosen, having been predestined according to the plan of him who works out everything in conformity with the purpose of his will."

Our inclusion in God's family is not an accident but is part of His divine plan. We were chosen and predestined according to God's purpose and will. This assurance provides us with confidence and security in our salvation.

Knowing that we are chosen according to God's plan gives us a deep sense of purpose and belonging. We are part of a divine narrative that spans from eternity past to eternity future.

Our lives have meaning and direction because they are woven into the fabric of God's redemptive plan. This should encourage us to live faithfully and confidently, knowing that God is at work in and through us.

For the praise of His glory ...

"In order that we, who were the first to put our hope in Christ, might be for the praise of his glory." Our salvation and the blessings we receive are ultimately for the praise of God's glory. Our lives are meant to reflect His greatness and bring Him honour. This purpose gives our lives meaning and direction, motivating us to live in a way that glorifies God.

The phrase *"for the praise of his glory"* occurs multiple times in Ephesians 1, underscoring its importance. God's ultimate goal in redemption is His own glory. As we live out our faith and experience the blessings of salvation, we bring glory to God. This is not an egotistical desire on God's part but a reflection of His worthiness and the proper response of creation to its Creator. When we live for God's glory, we find our highest joy and fulfillment.

Sealed with the Holy Spirit ...

"And you also were included in Christ when you heard the message of truth, the gospel of your salvation. When you believed, you were marked in him with a seal, the promised Holy Spirit, who is a deposit guaranteeing our inheritance until the redemption of those who are God's possession - to the praise of his glory."

The Holy Spirit is the seal and guarantee of our inheritance. When we believe in the gospel, we are marked with the Holy Spirit, who assures us of our future redemption and inheritance. This seal signifies that we belong to God and that He will fulfill His promises to us.

The imagery of sealing is significant. In the ancient world, a seal was used to mark ownership and to authenticate documents.

Similarly, the Holy Spirit marks us as God's own and assures us of our authentic relationship with Him. The Holy Spirit is also described as a "*deposit*" or "*down payment,*" guaranteeing that the full inheritance will be ours. This gives us great assurance and hope as we await the final redemption when Christ returns.

Practical Applications:

Embrace your identity in Christ ...

Reflect on the truth that you are chosen, adopted, redeemed, and forgiven in Christ. Embrace your identity as a child of God, and let this truth shape your self-image and your interactions with others. Remember that your worth and value are not based on your achievements or the opinions of others but on God's unchanging love and grace. Take time each day to remind yourself of your identity in Christ. Meditate on passages like Ephesians 1:3-14 and allow these truths to sink deeply into your heart and mind. Let your identity in Christ give you confidence and security as you face the challenges of life.

Live a life of holiness and blamelessness ...

Recognize that you have been chosen to live a holy and blameless life. Seek to honour God in your thoughts, words, and actions. Strive to live in a way that reflects the character of Christ and brings glory to God. Pursue spiritual disciplines that help you grow in holiness, such as prayer, Bible study, and worship. Surround yourself with fellow believers who encourage and support you in your journey of faith. Seek to live a life that is set apart for God's purposes and rely on the Holy Spirit to empower you to overcome sin and live in righteousness.

Celebrate your adoption into God's family ...

Rejoice in the fact that you have been adopted into God's family and enjoy the privileges and responsibilities that come with being a child of God. Celebrate the intimate relationship you have with your Heavenly Father and seek to deepen your connection with Him through prayer and worship.

Take time to reflect on the significance of your adoption. Consider how this truth impacts your sense of belonging and your relationship with others in the body of Christ. Celebrate your adoption by participating in the life of the church, serving others, and sharing the love of Christ with those around you.

Rest in the assurance of your redemption ...

Find comfort and peace in the knowledge that you have been redeemed and forgiven through the blood of Christ. Trust in the finished work of Christ on the cross, and rest in the assurance that your sins are forgiven and that you are reconciled to God.

Reflect on the significance of your redemption. Consider how this truth impacts your relationship with God and your daily life. Rest in the assurance of your redemption by continually turning to Christ in faith and relying on His grace to sustain you.

Seek to understand God's will ...

Cultivate a desire to know and understand the mystery of God's will. Spend time in prayer and study of God's Word, seeking to discern His purposes and plans for your life.

Trust that God, in His wisdom and understanding, will reveal His will to you in His perfect timing. Ask God to give you wisdom and understanding as you seek to know His will. Be open to the leading of the Holy Spirit, and be willing to follow God's direction, even when it requires faith and obedience. Trust that God's plans for you are good and that He is working all things together for His glory and your good.

Live for the praise of His glory ...

Remember that your life is meant to bring praise and glory to God. Seek to live in a way that reflects His greatness and honours His name. Let your actions, attitudes, and relationships be a testimony to the transformative power of the gospel. Consider how you can live for the praise of God's glory in your daily life. Look for opportunities to serve others, share the gospel, and demonstrate the love of Christ. Let your life be a reflection of God's grace and a testimony to His faithfulness.

Rely on the Holy Spirit ...

Depend on the Holy Spirit as your seal and guarantee of God's promises. Seek to be filled with the Spirit daily, allowing Him to guide, empower, and transform you. The Holy Spirit is your helper, comforter, and advocate, ensuring that you remain in God's grace.

Pray for the Holy Spirit's presence and power in your life. Ask Him to help you live out the truths of Ephesians 1:1-14, to grow in your relationship with Christ, and to bear fruit that brings glory to God. Trust that the Holy Spirit is at work in you, sealing you for the day of redemption and guaranteeing your inheritance in Christ.

Conclusion

In Ephesians 1:1-14, Paul presents a breathtaking view of the spiritual blessings we have in Christ. We are chosen, adopted, redeemed, and forgiven, all according to the riches of God's grace. These blessings are not just for our benefit but are ultimately for the praise of God's glory.

As we reflect on these truths, let us embrace our identity in Christ, live lives of holiness and love, and rely on the Holy Spirit to guide and empower us.

3. PRAYER FOR SPIRITUAL WISDOM

As we continue our journey through the book of Ephesians, we come to a passage that reveals Paul's heartfelt prayer for the believers in Ephesus. This is where Paul prays for the church to receive spiritual wisdom and revelation, to know God better, and to then understand the hope and power available to them in Christ.

> **Ephesians 1:15-23** *"For this reason, ever since I heard about your faith in the Lord Jesus and your love for all God's people, I have not stopped giving thanks for you, remembering you in my prayers. I keep asking that the God of our Lord Jesus Christ, the glorious Father, may give you the Spirit of wisdom and revelation, so that you may know him better.*
>
> *I pray that the eyes of your heart may be enlightened in order that you may know the hope to which he has called you, the riches of his glorious inheritance in his holy people, and his incomparably great power for us who believe. That power is the same as the mighty strength he exerted when he raised Christ from the dead and seated him at his right hand in the heavenly realms, far above all rule and authority, power and dominion, and every name that is invoked, not only in the present age but also in the one to come.*
>
> *And God placed all things under his feet and appointed him to be head over everything for the church, which is his body, the fullness of him who fills everything in every way."*

In this amazing passage, Paul expresses his gratitude for the Ephesian believers and prays that they may grow in their knowledge of God, understand the hope of their calling, and experience the greatness of God's power.

We will break down this passage into three main sections: Paul's thanksgiving and prayer (15-17), the enlightenment of the heart (18-19), and the exaltation of Christ (20-23).

Paul's thanksgiving and prayer (1:15-17)

Paul begins this section by expressing his gratitude for the faith and love of the Ephesian believers. He then outlines his specific prayer for them, asking God to grant them the Spirit of wisdom and revelation.

Thanksgiving for faith and love ...

"For this reason, ever since I heard about your faith in the Lord Jesus and your love for all God's people, I have not stopped giving thanks for you, remembering you in my prayers." Paul is deeply thankful for the faith and love of the Ephesians. Their faith in the Lord Jesus and love for all God's people are evidence of their genuine conversion and commitment to Christ.

Paul's gratitude is a reminder of the importance of recognizing and celebrating the faith and love in our own community. When we see others living out their faith and loving others, it should prompt us to give thanks and encourage them in their walk with Christ.

Prayer for the Spirit of wisdom and revelation ...

"I keep asking that the God of our Lord Jesus Christ, the glorious Father, may give you the Spirit of wisdom and revelation, so that you may know him better."

Paul's prayer is that the believers may receive the Spirit of wisdom and revelation to know God better. This prayer emphasizes the need for spiritual growth and a deeper relationship with God.

The Spirit of wisdom and revelation is essential for understanding the depths of God's character and His plans for our lives. Wisdom allows us to apply God's truth to our daily lives, while revelation provides insight into the mysteries of God. Together, they enable us to know God more intimately and to live in alignment with His will.

The enlightenment of the heart (1:18-19)

Paul continues his prayer by asking that the eyes of the believers' hearts may be enlightened. He wants them to grasp three specific truths: the hope of their calling, the riches of God's glorious inheritance, and the greatness of His power.

Knowing the hope of our calling ...

"I pray that the eyes of your heart may be enlightened in order that you may know the hope to which he has called you." Paul prays for the enlightenment of the heart so that believers may understand the hope of their calling. This hope is rooted in God's promises and in His eternal plan for us. The hope of our calling includes our future inheritance, eternal life, and the assurance of being with Christ forever. Understanding this hope gives us a sense of purpose and direction, motivating us to live faithfully and confidently in the present.

Understanding the riches of God's glorious inheritance ...

"The riches of his glorious inheritance in his holy people." Paul wants the believers to grasp the incredible value and richness of God's inheritance in them. This inheritance is not only what we receive from God but also how God views us as His treasured possession. Recognizing that we are God's inheritance gives us a profound sense of worth and significance.

It reminds us that we are deeply loved and valued by God, chosen to be His people and to share in His glory.

Experiencing the greatness of God's power ...

"And his incomparably great power for us who believe." Paul prays that believers may experience the greatness of God's power, which is available to us through faith. This power is the same mighty strength that raised Christ from the dead and seated Him at God's right hand.

Understanding and experiencing God's power is crucial for living a victorious Christian life. It enables us to overcome sin, endure trials, and fulfill God's purposes.

This power is not just a theological concept but a dynamic reality that transforms our lives. God's power and God's grace are one in the same. The best definition of 'grace' and one which is consistent with all the references to grace in the Bible, is 'God's empowering presence.' So, for Paul, to experience the reality of grace in our lives is to experience God's incomparably great power.

The exaltation of Christ (1:20-23)

Paul concludes this passage by highlighting the exaltation of Christ. He describes how God's power raised Christ from the dead, seated Him at His right hand, and appointed Him as the head of the church.

The resurrection and ascension of Christ ...

"That power is the same as the mighty strength he exerted when he raised Christ from the dead and seated him at his right hand in the heavenly realms." Paul emphasizes that the same power that raised Christ from the dead is available to believers.

The resurrection of Christ is the ultimate demonstration of God's power over sin and death. Christ's ascension to the right hand of God signifies His authority and sovereignty. He is exalted above all all rule, authority, power, and dominion. This position of honour reflects the fullness of His victory and the fulfillment of God's redemptive plan.

Christ's supremacy over all things ...

"Far above all rule and authority, power and dominion, and every name that is invoked, not only in the present age but also in the one to come." Christ's supremacy extends over all spiritual and earthly powers. He is exalted above every name and title, both now and in the future.

This supremacy assures us that Christ is in control and that nothing can thwart His purposes. It gives us confidence and security, knowing that our Saviour reigns over all things and that His authority is unchallenged.

Christ as Head of the Church ...

"And God placed all things under his feet and appointed him to be head over everything for the church, which is his body, the fullness of him who fills everything in every way." Paul concludes by affirming that Christ is the head of the church, His body.

The church is the fullness of Christ, Who fills everything in every way. As the head of the church, Christ provides leadership, direction, and sustenance. He unites and empowers His body, enabling us to carry out His mission on earth. Our identity and purpose as the church are rooted in our relationship with Christ, who fills us with His presence and power.

Practical Applications

Cultivate gratitude and prayer ...

I encourage you to reflect on Paul's example of thanksgiving and prayer for the believers. Take time to express gratitude for the faith and love of those in your church community. Make it a habit to pray for others, like Paul did here, asking God to give them spiritual wisdom and revelation.

Consider keeping a prayer diary where you record your prayers for others and the ways God answers them. Reflecting on these entries can help you cultivate a thankful heart and recognize God's faithfulness in your life. This practice can help you stay focused and intentional in your prayers, fostering a deeper sense of connection and intercession for your church family.

Find a prayer partner or join a prayer group where you can share prayer requests and pray for one another. This practice fosters accountability and encouragement in your prayer life. You should also incorporate thanksgiving into your personal and corporate worship times. Express gratitude to God for His blessings, His faithfulness, and the faith and love of your church community.

Seek spiritual wisdom and revelation ...

Pray for the Spirit of wisdom and revelation in your own life. Ask God to deepen your understanding of His character, His will and His purposes. Seek to know God better through prayer, Bible study, and meditation on His Word. Join a Bible study group or find a spiritual mentor who can help you grow in your knowledge of God. Engage in regular times of personal study and reflection, allowing the Holy Spirit to reveal new insights and truths to you.

Develop a personal study plan that includes regular Bible reading, reflection, and study. Choose a specific book of the Bible or a topic to explore in depth and seek God's wisdom and revelation as you study.

You could also set aside time for spiritual retreats or quiet days where you can focus on prayer, reflection, and seeking God's guidance. These times of intentional solitude can provide space for God to speak to you and reveal His will.

Embrace the hope of your calling ...

Reflect on the hope to which you have been called. Allow this hope to shape your perspective and priorities. Trust in God's promises and His eternal plan for your life, and let this assurance give you confidence and direction. Write down the specific promises of God that give you hope and meditate on them regularly. When faced with challenges or uncertainties, remind yourself of these promises and the hope you have in Christ.

Memorize key Scriptures that highlight the hope of your calling. Let these verses encourage and strengthen you, especially during times of difficulty or doubt and always look for opportunities to share the hope of your calling with others. Whether through conversations, testimonies, or acts of service, let your life be a beacon of hope to others.

Value your inheritance in Christ ...

Understand the richness of God's inheritance in you. Recognize your worth and significance as God's treasured possession. Let this truth give you a sense of purpose and motivate you to live a life that honours God. Reflect on how being part of God's inheritance affects your identity and your actions.

Consider how you can live out this identity in your relationships, work, and service. Celebrate your inheritance by sharing your faith and the love of Christ with others.

Write down some affirmations based on your identity in Christ and God's inheritance in you. Speak these affirmations daily to remind yourself of how God sees you and who you are in Christ.

Celebrate spiritual milestones and growth in your life and the lives of others. Acknowledge the ways God is working and the inheritance you share as His people.

Use your gifts and talents to serve others and build up the body of Christ. Recognize that your service is part of your inheritance and calling as a child of God.

Experience God's power ...

Seek to experience the greatness of God's power in your daily life. Depend on His strength to overcome challenges, resist temptation, and fulfill His purposes. Remember that the same power that raised Christ from the dead is available to you. Pray for God's empowering presence to be evident in specific areas of your life. Whether it is overcoming a particular sin, enduring a difficult situation, or stepping out in faith to serve - ask God to demonstrate His power in and through you.

Ask for His strength to overcome challenges, fulfill your calling, and demonstrate His love and grace to others and take steps of faith that require you to rely on God's power. Whether it's starting a new ministry, sharing your faith, or making a difficult decision, trust that God will empower you.

Share testimonies of God's power in your life with others. Encourage them with stories of how God has worked in and through you. This will inspire them to also trust in His power.

Recognize Christ's authority ...

Acknowledge Christ's supremacy and authority over all things. Trust in His sovereignty and control, even when circumstances seem uncertain or challenging. Let His authority give you confidence and peace. Reflect on areas of your life where you need to submit to Christ's authority.

Surrender your fears, plans, and decisions to Him, trusting that He is in control and will guide you according to His perfect will. Ask for His guidance and trust in His sovereignty, knowing that He is in control.

In decision-making, seek Christ's will through prayer, Scripture, and godly counsel. Trust that His authority will lead you in the right direction. Live with confidence and peace, knowing that Christ is supreme over all things. Let His authority give you assurance in the face of uncertainty and challenges.

Live as part of Christ's body ...

Embrace your role as a member of the body of Christ. Seek to contribute to the health and growth of the church by using the gifts God has awakened in you by serving others. Recognize that your identity and purpose are rooted in your relationship with Christ, the head of the church. Get involved in your local church by participating in ministries, small groups, and outreach opportunities. Look for ways to serve and support your church family, building up the body of Christ and reflecting His love to the world.

Identify and use your spiritual gifts to serve others and build up the church. Seek opportunities to minister and support your church community. Invest in building strong relationships within your church. Foster a sense of community and belonging, and encourage one another in your faith journeys.

Conclusion

In Ephesians 1:15-23, Paul expresses his gratitude for the Ephesian believers and prays that they may receive spiritual wisdom and revelation, understand the hope of their calling, and experience the greatness of God's power.

As we reflect on these vital truths, let us cultivate gratitude and prayer, seek to know God better, embrace our hope and inheritance in Christ, experience His power, recognize His authority, and live as part of His body.

4. ALIVE IN CHRIST

As we continue our study of Paul's letter to the Ephesians, we arrive at a passage that vividly contrasts our life before and after Christ. Paul describes our former state of spiritual death, our transformation through God's grace, and our new identity and purpose in Christ.

> **Ephesians 2:1-10** *"As for you, you were dead in your transgressions and sins, in which you used to live when you followed the ways of this world and of the ruler of the kingdom of the air, the spirit who is now at work in those who are disobedient. All of us also lived among them at one time, gratifying the cravings of our flesh and following its desires and thoughts. Like the rest, we were by nature deserving of wrath. But because of his great love for us, God, who is rich in mercy, made us alive with Christ even when we were dead in transgressions - it is by grace you have been saved.*
>
> *And God raised us up with Christ and seated us with him in the heavenly realms in Christ Jesus, in order that in the coming ages he might show the incomparable riches of his grace, expressed in his kindness to us in Christ Jesus. For it is by grace you have been saved, through faith - and this is not from yourselves, it is the gift of God - not by works, so that no one can boast. For we are God's handiwork, created in Christ Jesus to do good works, which God prepared in advance for us to do."*

This passage can be divided into three main sections: our condition before Christ (verses 1-3), our transformation through Christ (verses 4-7), and our new life and purpose in Christ (verses 8-10). Each section provides us with a profound understanding of God's grace and the radical change it brings to our lives.

Our condition before Christ (2:1-3)

Paul begins by describing the stark reality of our spiritual condition before we came to know Christ. He uses strong language to convey the depth of our lostness and the seriousness of our plight.

Dead in transgressions and sins ...

"*As for you, you were dead in your transgressions and sins.*" Paul uses the metaphor of death to describe our spiritual state apart from Christ. We were not just spiritually sick or weak; we were dead. Our transgressions and sins had completely separated us from the life of God.

Spiritual death means that we were unable to respond to God or seek Him on our own. Just as a physically dead person cannot revive themselves, so too, we are incapable of bringing ourselves back to life spiritually. This highlights the necessity of divine intervention and the power of God's grace.

Following the ways of the world ...

"*In which you used to live when you followed the ways of this world and of the ruler of the kingdom of the air, the spirit who is now at work in those who are disobedient.*" Our lives before Christ were marked by conformity to the patterns and values of the world. We followed the ways of the world, influenced by the ruler of the kingdom of the air, which refers to Satan.

The world and its values are often in direct opposition to God's kingdom. Before Christ, we were influenced and controlled by the spirit of disobedience, leading us away from God and into a life of sin.

Gratifying the cravings of the flesh ...

"All of us also lived among them at one time, gratifying the cravings of our flesh and following its desires and thoughts. Like the rest, we were by nature deserving of wrath." Our pre-Christian lives were characterized by a pursuit of selfish desires and sinful cravings. We followed the inclinations of our flesh, leading to actions and thoughts that were contrary to God's will.

This state of living according to the flesh made us deserving of God's wrath. God's wrath is His holy and just response to sin. It is not arbitrary or capricious but an inescapable aspect of His righteousness. Our sinful nature and actions placed us under His judgment.

Our transformation through Christ (2:4-7)

Paul then transitions from describing our former condition to highlighting the transformative power of God's grace. He explains how God's love and mercy have brought about a radical change in our lives.

Made alive with Christ ...

"But because of his great love for us, God, who is rich in mercy, made us alive with Christ even when we were dead in transgressions - it is by grace you have been saved." Despite our state of spiritual death, God's great love and rich mercy intervened. He made us alive with Christ, resurrecting us from our spiritual death.

This transformation is entirely due to God's grace. It is not something we earned or deserved or made happen in any way – it is a gift from God. His love and mercy motivated Him to rescue us from our hopeless condition and give us new life in Christ.

Raised and seated with Christ ...

"And God raised us up with Christ and seated us with him in the heavenly realms in Christ Jesus." Our union with Christ means that we share in His resurrection and exaltation. Just as Christ was raised from the dead and seated at the right hand of the Father, we too have been raised and seated with Him in the heavenly realms.

This positional truth signifies our new status and identity in Christ. We are no longer bound by the powers of this world but are seated with Christ in a place of authority and honour. This gives us a new perspective and empowers us to live victoriously.

Demonstration of God's grace ...

"In order that in the coming ages he might show the incomparable riches of his grace, expressed in his kindness to us in Christ Jesus." In transforming us, God displays the incomparable riches of His grace. Our lives become a testimony to His kindness and the greatness of His grace. Throughout eternity, God's grace will be on display through the lives of those He has redeemed.

This demonstrates His character and brings glory to His name. Our transformation is not just for our benefit but also to reveal God's grace and power to the world.

Our new life and purpose in Christ (2:8-10)

Paul concludes this passage by emphasizing the nature of our salvation and our new purpose in Christ. He highlights that our salvation is by grace through faith and that we are created for good works.

Saved by grace through faith ...

"For it is by grace you have been saved, through faith - and this is not from yourselves, it is the gift of God - not by works, so that no one can boast." Paul reiterates that our salvation is entirely by grace through faith. It is a gift from God, not something we can achieve through our own efforts. This truth eliminates any basis for boasting. We cannot take credit for our salvation because it is a work of God's grace from start to finish. Our response is simply to receive this gift by faith, trusting in what Christ has done for us.

God's handiwork ...

"For we are God's handiwork, created in Christ Jesus to do good works, which God prepared in advance for us to do." Our new identity in Christ means that we are God's handiwork, His masterpiece. We have been created anew in Christ Jesus with a specific purpose: to do good works. These good works are not the basis of our salvation but the result of it. They are the evidence of our new life in Christ and the fruit of God's transforming grace. God has prepared these works in advance for us to walk in, giving our lives purpose.

Practical Applications

Ephesians 2:1-10 is a profound passage, focusing on the transformation from spiritual death to life in Christ, by God's grace. Here are some obvious practical applications:

Recognize your past condition ...

"As for you, you were dead in your transgressions and sins, in which you used to live when you followed the ways of this world and of the ruler of the kingdom of the air, the spirit who is now at work in those who are disobedient." (2:1-2)

Before knowing Christ, we were spiritually dead, incapable of living the life God designed for us. Paul reminds us that without Christ, our condition was not just flawed but dead - spiritually lifeless. Recognizing this past reality is crucial for developing a deeper sense of humility and gratitude. It highlights the stark contrast between life before Christ and life after Christ, reminding us of the seriousness of sin and our desperate need for salvation.

Regularly reflecting on your past condition can create a deep sense of thankfulness and humility. It is important to understand where you came from, spiritually speaking, to appreciate the depth of God's mercy.

This should move you to greater compassion toward others who are still lost in their sin. Instead of being judgmental, we are reminded that we, too, were once in exactly the same place, following the ways of the world, until God intervened and made us alive in Christ.

Take time to journal or reflect on your spiritual journey - the moments where you felt far from God, how He brought you out, and the transformation that took place. Consider sharing this testimony with someone who may be struggling in their own journey. This can encourage them to see God's power to change lives.

Acknowledge God's grace and love ...

"But because of his great love for us, God, who is rich in mercy, made us alive with Christ even when we were dead in transgressions - it is by grace you have been saved." (2:4-5)

Paul shifts the focus from humanity's deadness in sin to God's great love and mercy. Our salvation is entirely dependent on God's grace, not on any merit of our own.

This is a key truth for believers, as it shapes how we see our relationship with God. We didn't earn our way into God's favour - He extended it freely out of love. This recognition should always stir up profound gratitude in us and a reliance on God's grace every day of our lives.

Acknowledge that it's solely because of God's love and grace that you are saved. There is nothing you could have done to deserve it. This should lead you to embrace a life of worship, praise, and gratitude. It also encourages you to extend grace to others because God first extended grace to you. Begin each day with a prayer of thanksgiving. Make it a daily habit to thank God for His mercy and grace. Also, look for opportunities to show grace to others in your life. This could mean forgiving someone who has wronged you or helping someone without expecting anything in return.

Live in the reality of new life ...

"And God raised us up with Christ and seated us with him in the heavenly realms in Christ Jesus." (2:6)

This passage emphasizes that believers are not just spiritually alive; we are seated with Christ in heavenly realms. This is a powerful declaration of the believer's new identity and status. Although we live in this earthly kingdom, we are now also citizens of the kingdom of heaven, and our spiritual position in Christ is secure. Living in this reality should affect how we approach our daily lives - from how we interact with others to how we respond to challenges.

Embrace your new life and identity in Christ. You are no longer defined by your past mistakes or sins but by the life of Christ living within you. This realization gives you confidence to live out your faith boldly and victoriously.

Make a conscious effort to live out your new identity in Christ every day in every part of your life. This could involve starting the day by meditating on scriptures that affirm who you are in Christ (e.g., 2 Corinthians 5:17). Engage in spiritual disciplines like prayer, Bible reading, and fellowship with other believers to remind yourself of your heavenly position and live accordingly.

Boast in God, not yourself ...

"For it is by grace you have been saved, through faith - and this is not from yourselves, it is the gift of God - not by works, so that no one can boast." (2:8-9)

Salvation is a gift from God, given by grace and received through faith. It is not something we can achieve by our own efforts, so we have no grounds to boast about our salvation. This truth should humble us, reminding us that we are entirely dependent on God for our salvation. It also challenges any self-righteous tendencies, pushing us to continually point others to God's grace rather than our own works or achievements.

So, keep your heart focused on God's grace, and resist the temptation to take credit for your salvation or spiritual growth. Always give glory to God for what He has done in your life. When people commend you for your spiritual progress or good deeds, develop the habit of redirecting the praise back to God. Share with others how it is God's grace working in and through you that enables you to live a life of faith.

Understand you are created for good works ...

"For we are God's handiwork, created in Christ Jesus to do good works, which God prepared in advance for us to do." (2:10)

As believers, we are God's handiwork, His masterpiece, created for a purpose. We are not saved by good works, but we are saved for good works. This means that our lives should reflect God's purposes and plans. These good works are not arbitrary but are prepared by God in advance. Every believer has a specific role to play in God's kingdom, and we are called to live it out.

Embrace the truth that your life has a divine purpose. You were created to make a positive impact in the world through the good works that God has planned for you. This should motivate you to seek out ways to serve others, contribute to the church, and live out your faith in tangible ways. Ask God to reveal the specific good works He has prepared for you.

Take time to reflect on your gifts, talents, and passions, and look for ways to use them in service to others. This could involve volunteering in your church or community, mentoring someone, or using your skills to help those in need.

Embrace humility and service ...

Knowing that you are saved by grace should inspire a life of humility. There is no room for arrogance in the Christian life. Instead, we should view ourselves as servants, seeking to build up others rather than ourselves. Christ set the example of humility and service, and we are called to follow His lead. Cultivate a servant heart by looking for opportunities to bless and give to others in your daily life.

This might mean helping a neighbour, volunteering for a cause, or offering encouragement to someone in need. Make it a goal to serve without seeking recognition or praise.

Trust in God's power to transform ...

The same power that raised Christ from the dead is at work in you. This should give you confidence that God is continually transforming you, even in areas where you struggle. Trust that God is working in your life, sanctifying you and making you more like Christ. When facing difficulties or areas of personal weakness, remind yourself of God's power to transform.

Approach these challenges with faith, trusting that God is not done with you yet. You may even create a specific prayer journal where you write down the areas you are asking God to transform you and document how He is answering those prayers over time.

Conclusion

The practical applications of Ephesians 2:1-10 are life-changing and relevant for daily Christian living. As we reflect on these truths, let us recognize the reality of spiritual death, embrace God's grace, live out our new identity, be a testimony of His grace, and engage in the good works He has prepared for us. May we carry these truths in our hearts and live out our faith boldly and joyfully.

5. UNITY IN CHRIST

We now come to a passage that highlights the unity we have in Christ, as Paul addresses the division between Jews and Gentiles and how Christ has reconciled both groups into one body, creating a new humanity and establishing peace.

> **Ephesians 2:11-22** *"Therefore, remember that formerly you who are Gentiles by birth and called 'uncircumcised' by those who call themselves 'the circumcision' (which is done in the body by human hands) - remember that at that time you were separate from Christ, excluded from citizenship in Israel and foreigners to the covenants of the promise, without hope and without God in the world. But now in Christ Jesus you who once were far away have been brought near by the blood of Christ.*
>
> *For he himself is our peace, who has made the two groups one and has destroyed the barrier, the dividing wall of hostility, by setting aside in his flesh the law with its commands and regulations. His purpose was to create in himself one new humanity out of the two, thus making peace, and in one body to reconcile both of them to God through the cross, by which he put to death their hostility. He came and preached peace to you who were far away and peace to those who were near. For through him we both have access to the Father by one Spirit.*
>
> *Consequently, you are no longer foreigners and strangers, but fellow citizens with God's people and also members of his household, built on the foundation of the apostles and prophets, with Christ Jesus himself as the chief cornerstone. In him the whole building is joined together and rises to become a holy temple in the Lord. And in him you too are being built together to become a dwelling in which God lives by his Spirit."*

This passage is divided into three main sections: the former state of the Gentiles (verses 11-12), the reconciliation through Christ (verses 13-18), and the new community in Christ (verses 19-22). Each section provides us with profound insights into the nature of our unity in Christ and the peace He brings.

The former state of the Gentiles (2:11-12)

Paul begins by reminding the Gentile believers of their former state before coming to Christ. He emphasizes their separation from God and the Jewish people.

Gentiles by birth ...

"Therefore, remember that formerly you who are Gentiles by birth and called 'uncircumcised' by those who call themselves 'the circumcision' (which is done in the body by human hands)."

Paul addresses the Gentile believers, reminding them of their past identity as *"Gentiles by birth."* They were considered *"uncircumcised"* by the Jews, who took pride in their physical circumcision as a sign of their covenant with God. The term "uncircumcised" was often used derogatorily by the Jews to describe the Gentiles. It highlighted the physical and cultural distinction between the two groups. This distinction created a significant barrier and a sense of superiority among the Jews.

Separation from Christ and Israel ...

"Remember that at that time you were separate from Christ, excluded from citizenship in Israel and foreigners to the covenants of the promise, without hope and without God in the world." Paul emphasizes the spiritual and social separation the Gentiles experienced.

They were separate from Christ, excluded from the community of Israel, and strangers to the covenants of promise. This separation meant that the Gentiles were without hope and without God in the world. They did not have access to the promises and blessings that were part of God's covenant with Israel. Their exclusion left them in a state of spiritual alienation and hopelessness.

The reconciliation through Christ (2:13-18)

Paul then transitions to the transformative work of Christ, highlighting how He has reconciled both Jews and Gentiles through His sacrifice.

Brought near by the blood of Christ ...

"But now in Christ Jesus you who once were far away have been brought near by the blood of Christ." Paul contrasts the former state of the Gentiles with their new reality in Christ. Through the blood of Christ, those who were once far away have been brought near. This nearness signifies a restored relationship with God and inclusion in His covenant community.

The blood of Christ refers to His sacrificial death on the cross. It is through His atoning sacrifice that the barrier of sin is removed, and reconciliation with God is made possible. This act of grace extends to all people, regardless of their ethnic or cultural background.

Christ as our peace ...

"For he himself is our peace, who has made the two groups one and has destroyed the barrier, the dividing wall of hostility." Christ is described as our peace, the one who has made peace possible by reconciling the two groups - Jews and Gentiles - into one. He has destroyed the barrier, the dividing wall of hostility, that separated them.

The "*dividing wall of hostility*" likely refers to the ceremonial and legal distinctions that separated Jews and Gentiles. By setting aside the law with its commands and regulations, Christ has removed the barriers that caused division and enmity. His purpose was to create a new, unified humanity.

One new humanity ...

"*His purpose was to create in himself one new humanity out of the two, thus making peace, and in one body to reconcile both of them to God through the cross, by which he put to death their hostility.*" Christ's reconciling work goes beyond individual salvation; it includes the creation of a new, unified community.

This new humanity is characterized by peace and reconciliation, both with God and with one another. Through the cross, Christ has put to death the hostility that existed between Jews and Gentiles. He has reconciled both groups to God in one body, creating a new community where unity and peace prevail. This new humanity is not defined by ethnic or cultural distinctions but by a shared identity in Christ.

Preaching peace ...

"He came and preached peace to you who were far away and peace to those who were near. For through him we both have access to the Father by one Spirit." Christ's message of peace extends to both those who were far away (Gentiles) and those who were near (Jews).

Through Him, both groups have access to the Father by one Spirit. This access is a profound privilege made possible by the Holy Spirit. It signifies a restored relationship with God and the breaking down of barriers that separated humanity. In Christ, all believers, regardless of their background, are brought into a unified relationship with God.

The new community in Christ (2:19-22)

Paul concludes by describing the new community that has been formed in Christ. He uses several metaphors to illustrate the unity and significance of this new community.

Fellow citizens and members of God's household ...

"*Consequently, you are no longer foreigners and strangers, but fellow citizens with God's people and also members of his household.*" Paul emphasizes the change in the Gentiles' status. They are no longer outsiders but are now fellow citizens with God's people and members of His household. This metaphor of citizenship highlights the inclusion and belonging that comes with being part of God's kingdom.

As members of God's household, believers are part of a spiritual family with God as their Father. This new identity brings with it privileges and responsibilities as part of God's people.

Built on the foundation of the Apostles and Prophets ...

"*Built on the foundation of the apostles and prophets, with Christ Jesus himself as the chief cornerstone.*" Paul uses the metaphor of a building to describe the new community.

The foundation of this building is the teaching of the apostles and prophets, with Christ Jesus as the chief cornerstone.

The cornerstone is the most important stone in a building, providing stability and alignment. Christ, as the chief cornerstone, ensures the integrity and unity of the entire structure. The apostles and prophets laid the foundational teachings upon which the church is built.

A holy temple in the Lord ...

"In him the whole building is joined together and rises to become a holy temple in the Lord." The new community is likened to a holy temple, joined together in Christ and rising to become a dwelling place for God.

This temple is not a physical structure but a spiritual one, made up of believers who are united in Christ. The imagery of a temple emphasizes the sacredness and holiness of the community. As God's dwelling place, the church is set apart for His purposes and reflects His glory. This unity and holiness are essential aspects of the new humanity created in Christ.

A dwelling for God's Spirit ...

"And in him you too are being built together to become a dwelling in which God lives by his Spirit." Paul concludes by affirming that believers are being built together to become a dwelling place for God's Spirit. This ongoing process of being built together emphasizes the continuous work of the Holy Spirit in the life of the church.

As a dwelling place for God's Spirit, the church is empowered and guided by the Holy Spirit. This divine presence ensures that the church remains united, holy, and effective in its mission. The presence of the Holy Spirit is a testament to the transformative power of God's grace.

Practical Applications

Embrace your identity in Christ ...

Reflect on the profound truth that you are no longer a foreigner or stranger but a fellow citizen and member of God's household.

Embrace your new identity in Christ and let it shape your sense of belonging and purpose. Take time to meditate on the significance of being part of God's kingdom and family. Allow this truth to give you confidence and security, knowing that you are deeply loved and valued by God.

Spend time in personal reflection and prayer, asking God to help you fully embrace your new identity in Christ. Reflect on the ways God has transformed your life and give thanks for His grace and love. Engage in a study of Scriptures that highlight your identity in Christ.

Passages like Ephesians 2:11-22, 1 Peter 2:9-10, and Romans 8:14-17 can help deepen your understanding of who you are in Christ. You could also write down some affirmations based on your new identity in Christ and speak them daily. Let these affirmations remind you of your worth, value, and belonging as a member of God's family.

Pursue unity and reconciliation ...

Recognize the importance of unity and reconciliation within the body of Christ. Seek to break down any barriers or divisions that may exist within your church or community. Pursue peace and reconciliation, both with God and with others. Reflect on areas where there may be division or hostility in your relationships or community.

Take intentional steps to promote understanding, forgiveness, and unity. Pray for God's grace and wisdom to navigate these challenges and to build a more unified and loving community.

Practice healthy conflict resolution in your relationships. When conflicts arise, seek to address them with grace, humility, and a desire for reconciliation. Use biblical principles of peacemaking, such as those found in Matthew 18:15-17 and Romans 12:18. Promote diversity and inclusion within your church and community. Celebrate the variety of unique backgrounds and cultures of those around you and seek to create an environment where everyone feels valued and included.

Get involved in initiatives that promote unity. Whether it's through community outreach, social justice efforts, or interfaith dialogues, look for ways to be a catalyst for healing and reconciliation.

Live out your new humanity ...

Live out your new identity as part of the new humanity created in Christ. Let go of old prejudices, biases, and divisions, and embrace the unity and peace that Christ has established. Reflect the love and grace of Christ in your interactions with others. Consider how you can be a peacemaker and a bridge-builder in your community. Look for opportunities to connect with people from different backgrounds and cultures and seek to build relationships based on mutual respect and understanding.

Engage with people from different cultures and different backgrounds. Learn about their experiences, perspectives, and traditions, and seek to build meaningful relationships based on mutual respect and understanding. Demonstrate the love and grace of Christ through acts of kindness and service. Look for opportunities to serve others and to be a blessing to those around you. Participate in community-building activities that foster unity and connection.
Whether it's through church events, neighbourhood gatherings, or volunteer opportunities, seek to build a sense of community and belonging.

Build on the foundation of Christ ...

Ensure that your life and faith are built on the foundation of Christ and the teachings of the apostles and prophets. Study God's Word diligently and seek to apply its truths to your life. Let Christ be the cornerstone of your faith, providing stability and alignment. Engage in regular personal Bible study and seek to grow in your understanding of God's Word. Surround yourself with sound teaching and seek the guidance of mature believers who can help you build a strong foundation in your faith.

Make Bible study a regular part of your routine. Join a Bible study group that helps you grow in your understanding of God's Word. Seek out sound teaching and preaching that is grounded in Scripture. Listen to sermons, podcasts, and teachings that help you build a strong foundation in your faith. Find a spiritual mentor who can guide you in your faith journey. Seek the wisdom and guidance of mature believers who can help you build a strong foundation in Christ.

Understanding the depth of reconciliation in Christ

To fully appreciate the reconciliation that Christ brings, we need to delve deeper into its theological and practical implications.

Theological implications ...

Reconciliation in Christ is not just about mending human relationships; it is first and foremost about restoring our relationship with God.
Sin created a barrier between humanity and God, but through Christ's sacrificial death, that barrier has been removed. We are now reconciled to God, and this reconciliation forms the basis for our unity with others.

This reconciliation is comprehensive, affecting every aspect of our lives. It transforms our identity, our relationships, and our purpose. It brings us into a new community where peace, unity, and love prevail.

Practical implications ...

Reconciliation in Christ calls us to be peacemakers and bridge-builders. It challenges us to break down the barriers that divide us and to seek unity and harmony in our relationships. It requires us to address issues of injustice, prejudice, and discrimination, and to work towards healing and reconciliation in our communities.

This reconciliation also calls us to live out the values of God's kingdom - values of love, grace, mercy, and justice. It invites us to participate in God's redemptive work in the world, bringing His message of reconciliation to those who are far off and those who are near.

Living as a unified body in Christ ...

The unity we have in Christ is not just a theological concept; it is a lived reality that shapes how we interact with one another and how we function as the body of Christ. Unity requires intentional effort and commitment. It involves actively working to build relationships, promote understanding, and address conflicts. It calls us to prioritize the well-being of the community over our individual preferences and to seek the common good.

Unity in Christ does not mean uniformity; it means celebrating the diversity of gifts, backgrounds, and perspectives within the whole body of Christ. It means recognizing that our differences enrich the community and reflect the multifaceted nature of God's creation. Unity is expressed through our collective service and mission. As the body of Christ, we are called to work together to advance God's kingdom and to serve those in need. This collaborative effort requires humility, cooperation, and a shared vision.

Conclusion

In Ephesians 2:11-22, Paul presents a powerful vision of unity in Christ. He reminds us of our former state of separation, the reconciliation we have through Christ, and the new community we are part of in Him. As we reflect on these truths, let us embrace our identity in Christ, pursue unity and reconciliation, live out our new humanity, build on the foundation of Christ, and be a dwelling for God's Spirit.

6. THE MYSTERY REVEALED

In the first 13 verses of Ephesians chapter 3, the Apostle Paul explains the mystery that has been revealed to him, a mystery that has profound implications for both Jews and Gentiles.

> **Ephesians 3:1-13** *"For this reason I, Paul, the prisoner of Christ Jesus for the sake of you Gentiles - surely you have heard about the administration of God's grace that was given to me for you, that is, the mystery made known to me by revelation, as I have already written briefly. In reading this, then, you will be able to understand my insight into the mystery of Christ, which was not made known to people in other generations as it has now been revealed by the Spirit to God's holy apostles and prophets. This mystery is that through the gospel the Gentiles are heirs together with Israel, members together of one body, and sharers together in the promise in Christ Jesus.*
>
> *I became a servant of this gospel by the gift of God's grace given me through the working of his power. Although I am less than the least of all the Lord's people, this grace was given me: to preach to the Gentiles the boundless riches of Christ, and to make plain to everyone the administration of this mystery, which for ages past was kept hidden in God, who created all things.*
>
> *His intent was that now, through the church, the manifold wisdom of God should be made known to the rulers and authorities in the heavenly realms, according to his eternal purpose that he accomplished in Christ Jesus our Lord. In him and through faith in him we may approach God with freedom and confidence. I ask you, therefore, not to be discouraged because of my sufferings for you, which are your glory."*

This passage can be divided into three main sections: Paul's explanation of his ministry and the mystery of Christ (verses 1-6), the purpose and power of his ministry (verses 7-10), and the confidence and encouragement for believers (verses 11-13). Each section provides us with profound insights into the nature of the gospel and our relationship with God through Christ.

Paul's ministry and the mystery of Christ (3:1-6)

Paul begins by explaining his role as a servant of the gospel and the mystery that has been revealed to him. This mystery, previously hidden, has now been made known through the Spirit.

"For this reason, I, Paul, the prisoner of Christ Jesus for the sake of you Gentiles..." Paul identifies himself as a prisoner of Christ Jesus. At the time of writing, Paul was literally in prison, likely in Rome, because of his ministry to the Gentiles.

However, he sees himself as a prisoner not of Rome but of Christ, indicating his complete dedication to the cause of Christ. Paul's imprisonment underscores the cost of discipleship and the commitment required to follow Christ. It also highlights the seriousness with which Paul takes his calling to minister to the Gentiles.

The administration of God's grace ...

Paul speaks of the special stewardship or administration of God's grace entrusted to him. *"Surely you have heard about the administration of God's grace that was given to me for you, that is, the mystery made known to me by revelation, as I have already written briefly."* This grace involves the revelation of a mystery that was previously hidden.

This mystery, revealed by God, is central to Paul's ministry. It is a divine revelation that has been made known to Paul and other apostles and prophets by the Spirit.

The mystery of Christ ...

Paul refers to his insight into the mystery of Christ, a mystery that was not revealed to previous generations but has now been made known through the Spirit. *"In reading this, then, you will be able to understand my insight into the mystery of Christ, which was not made known to people in other generations as it has now been revealed by the Spirit to God's holy apostles and prophets."* This mystery, as Paul explains, is that the Gentiles are now fellow heirs, members of the same body, and partakers of the promise in Christ Jesus through the gospel. This was a radical and revolutionary revelation that broke down the long-standing barriers between Jews and Gentiles.

Unity in the Gospel ...

"This mystery is that through the gospel the Gentiles are heirs together with Israel, members together of one body, and sharers together in the promise in Christ Jesus." The mystery revealed is the inclusion of the Gentiles in the promises and blessings of God. Through the gospel, Gentiles and Jews are united as heirs, members, and sharers together in Christ. This unity is a profound demonstration of God's grace and the power of the gospel to break down barriers and create a new, inclusive community in Christ.

The purpose and power of Paul's ministry (3:7-10)

Paul continues by describing the purpose and power behind his ministry. He emphasizes the grace given to him and the responsibility to make the mystery of Christ known.

A servant of the Gospel ...

"I became a servant of this gospel by the gift of God's grace given me through the working of his power." Paul describes himself as a servant of the gospel, a role given to him by God's grace and empowered by God's working. His ministry is not based on his own abilities but on the grace and power of God. This highlights the humility and dependence required in ministry. It is God's power at work in and through us that enables us to fulfill our calling.

Preaching the boundless riches of Christ ...

"Although I am less than the least of all the Lord's people, this grace was given me: to preach to the Gentiles the boundless riches of Christ." Paul humbly acknowledges his unworthiness but emphasizes the grace given to him to preach the boundless riches of Christ.

The riches of Christ refer to the immeasurable blessings and treasures available to believers through Christ. Paul's preaching is focused on revealing the vast and boundless blessings that come from a relationship with Christ. These riches include salvation, forgiveness, eternal life, and the indwelling presence of the Holy Spirit.

Making the mystery plain ...

"And to make plain to everyone the administration of this mystery, which for ages past was kept hidden in God, who created all things." Paul's mission is to make the mystery of Christ plain to everyone. This mystery, hidden for ages, is now revealed and must be proclaimed to all. The revelation of this mystery demonstrates God's sovereign plan and purpose. It was hidden in God, the Creator of all things, and has now been made known through the gospel.

The manifold wisdom of God ...

"His intent was that now, through the church, the manifold wisdom of God should be made known to the rulers and authorities in the heavenly realms." God's purpose in revealing this mystery is to display His manifold wisdom through the church. The church, as the body of Christ, is the instrument through which God's wisdom is made known to the spiritual rulers and authorities. The term *"manifold wisdom"* suggests the multifaceted and diverse nature of God's wisdom. It is displayed in the unity and diversity of the church, reflecting God's grand design and purpose.

3. Confidence and encouragement for believers (3:11-13)

Paul concludes this section by offering confidence and encouragement to believers. He emphasizes the access we have to God and the boldness we can have in Christ.

God's eternal purpose ...

"According to his eternal purpose that he accomplished in Christ Jesus our Lord." The revelation of the mystery and the inclusion of the Gentiles are part of God's eternal purpose, accomplished in Christ Jesus. This eternal purpose reflects God's sovereign plan for redemption and reconciliation. Knowing that our inclusion in God's family is part of His eternal purpose gives us confidence and assurance. It reminds us that our salvation is not an afterthought but a central part of God's redemptive plan.

Access to God ...

"In him and through faith in him we may approach God with freedom and confidence." Through Christ, we have direct access to God.

We can approach Him with freedom and confidence, knowing that we are accepted and loved. This access is a profound privilege that was made possible by Christ's sacrifice. It signifies a restored relationship with God, where we can come to Him without fear or hesitation.

Encouragement in suffering ...

"I ask you, therefore, not to be discouraged because of my sufferings for you, which are your glory." Paul concludes by encouraging the believers not to be discouraged by his sufferings. His imprisonment and hardships are for their benefit and glory. Paul's perspective on suffering serves to challenge us to view difficulties and trials through the lens of God's purpose. His sufferings are not in vain but will become part of God's plan to advance the gospel and build the church.

Practical Applications

Embrace the mystery of Christ ...

Reflect on the profound mystery of Christ revealed through the gospel. Embrace the inclusivity of the gospel and the unity it brings among believers. Recognize that in Christ, there are no barriers of race, ethnicity, or background. Take time to meditate on the unity we have in Christ. Consider how this unity can shape your interactions with others and your involvement in the church.

Consider how this truth impacts your view of others and your role in the church. Reflect on the ways you can promote unity and inclusivity in your relationships and community. Engage in conversations and activities that promote diversity and inclusion within your church and community.

Celebrate the unique backgrounds and perspectives of others and seek to build meaningful relationships based on mutual respect and understanding.

Participate in initiatives that promote unity within the body of Christ. Whether it's through community service projects, interfaith dialogues, or church events, look for ways to build bridges and promote understanding.

Depend on God's grace and power ...

Like Paul, acknowledge your dependence on God's grace and power in your life and ministry. Recognize that it is not your abilities or efforts but God's grace that enables you to serve and fulfill your calling. Pray for God's grace and power to be evident in your life. Regularly pray for God's grace and power to be evident in your life. Acknowledge your dependence on Him and seek His strength in every aspect of your ministry and daily life.

Cultivate a posture of humility and dependence on God. Recognize that it is not your abilities or efforts but God's grace that enables you to serve and fulfill your calling. Seek to glorify God in all that you do. Share testimonies of God's grace and power in your life with others. Encourage others by sharing how God has worked in and through you and inspire them to trust in His grace.

Proclaim the boundless riches of Christ ...

Commit to sharing the boundless riches of Christ with others. Recognize the immeasurable blessings you have received in Christ and seek to make them known to those around you. Whether through personal conversations, small group discussions, or public speaking, let the message of Christ's riches flow from your life.

Be intentional about sharing your personal testimony. Prepare a brief version of your story that highlights the key moments of your transformation and the impact of God's grace. Demonstrate the boundless riches of Christ through acts of service and kindness. Look for opportunities to serve others and to be a blessing to those around you.

Let your actions be a testimony to the love and grace of Christ. Look for opportunities to have gospel-centred conversations with others. Whether through casual conversations, small group discussions, or public speaking, seek to share the message of Christ's riches with those around you.

Demonstrate God's manifold wisdom ...

Seek to display the manifold wisdom of God through your life and the life of your church. Embrace the diversity and unity within the body of Christ and reflect God's wisdom in your relationships and actions. Celebrate the unique gifts and perspectives of others and work together to advance God's kingdom.

Engage with your community in ways that reflect God's manifold wisdom. Participate in community events, volunteer opportunities, and initiatives that promote unity and diversity.

Approach God with confidence ...

Take advantage of the access you have to God through Christ. Approach Him with freedom and confidence, knowing that you are loved and accepted. Bring your needs, concerns, and praises to Him in prayer. Make prayer a central part of your daily life. Develop a habit of coming to God with confidence, trusting in His love and faithfulness.

Set aside some dedicated times for prayer each day, and throughout the day, maintain a posture of openness to God's presence and guidance. Keep a prayer journal where you record your prayers, reflections, and how God answers them. This practice can help you see God's faithfulness over time and encourage you to approach Him with even greater confidence.

Meditate on Scriptures that emphasize God's accessibility and love. Verses like Hebrews 4:16, *"Let us then approach God's throne of grace with confidence, so that we may receive mercy and find grace to help us in our time of need,"* can strengthen your faith and encourage you to come boldly before God.

Find strength in suffering ...

When facing difficulties and trials, remember Paul's example and find strength in knowing that your sufferings are not in vain. Trust that God is at work in and through your hardships to accomplish His purposes. Reflect on how God has used past sufferings to grow and strengthen you. Find encouragement in knowing that He is with you in your current challenges and will use them for His glory. Reflect on Paul's example and his perspective on suffering.

Understand that suffering can be a part of God's plan to accomplish His purposes. See your trials as opportunities for growth and deeper dependence on God. Build a support network of fellow believers who can encourage and pray for you during times of suffering. Share your struggles with some trusted friends or mentors and allow them to walk alongside you. Continually remind yourself of God's faithfulness and sovereignty. Trust that He is with you in your suffering and will use it for His glory and your good.

Reflect on Romans 8:28, which assures us that "*in all things God works for the good of those who love him, who have been called according to his purpose.*"

Theological reflections on the mystery of Christ

To further understand the depth of the mystery of Christ revealed in Ephesians 3:1-13, let's delve into some theological reflections.

The nature of the mystery ...

The term "*mystery*" in the New Testament often refers to something that was previously hidden but has now been revealed. In this context, the mystery is that Gentiles are now fully included in God's redemptive plan. This inclusion was not fully understood in previous generations but has now been made clear through Christ and the apostles.

Revelation through the Spirit ...

The mystery of Christ was revealed by the Holy Spirit to the apostles and prophets. This underscores the role of the Holy Spirit in guiding and revealing God's truth. The Spirit's work is essential for understanding and proclaiming the gospel.

Unity in diversity ...

The inclusion of the Gentiles highlights the unity and diversity of the body of Christ. God's redemptive plan is inclusive, breaking down ethnic, cultural, and social barriers. This unity in diversity reflects the heart of God and His desire for all people to be reconciled to Him and to each other.

The Church as a witness ...

The church, as the body of Christ, is the instrument through which God's manifold wisdom is displayed. The unity and diversity within the church serve as a powerful witness to the world and to the spiritual realms. It demonstrates God's redemptive power and His ability to bring harmony out of diversity.

Living out the mystery of Christ ...

Understanding the mystery of Christ and its implications should lead to practical changes in how we live and interact with others. Actively work to include others in your church and community. Reach out to people from different backgrounds and cultures, seeking to build inclusive and welcoming environments. Reflect the inclusive nature of the gospel in your actions and attitudes.

Recognize and celebrate the unity and diversity within the body of Christ. Participate in events and activities that highlight different cultures and perspectives. Embrace the richness that diversity brings to the church and the community.

Let your life be a witness to the unity and love of Christ. Demonstrate through your actions and relationships the power of the gospel to break down barriers and create a new community. Share the message of Christ's inclusive love with those around you.

Engage in service and mission work that reflects the unity and diversity of the church. Serve alongside people from different backgrounds and experiences, and work together to advance God's kingdom. Let your collective efforts be a testimony to the world of the transformative power of the gospel.

Conclusion

In Ephesians 3:1-13, Paul reveals the profound mystery of Christ, emphasizing the inclusivity of the gospel and the unity it brings among believers. He explains his role in making this mystery known and encourages believers to approach God with confidence and not to be discouraged by his sufferings.

As we reflect on these truths, let us embrace the mystery of Christ, depend on God's grace and power, proclaim the boundless riches of Christ, demonstrate God's manifold wisdom, approach God with confidence, and find strength in suffering.

May we live out these truths in our daily lives, promoting unity and inclusivity, and being a witness to the transformative power of the gospel.

7. PAUL'S PRAYER

In the final verses of Ephesians 3, Paul prays for the church to be strengthened with power, for them to grasp the depth of Christ's love, and to be filled with the fullness of God. This prayer reveals Paul's deep pastoral care and his desire for the spiritual maturity and empowerment of all believers.

> **Ephesians 3:14-21** *"For this reason I kneel before the Father, from whom every family in heaven and on earth derives its name. I pray that out of his glorious riches he may strengthen you with power through his Spirit in your inner being, so that Christ may dwell in your hearts through faith.*
>
> *And I pray that you, being rooted and established in love, may have power, together with all the Lord's holy people, to grasp how wide and long and high and deep is the love of Christ, and to know this love that surpasses knowledge - that you may be filled to the measure of all the fullness of God.*
>
> *Now to him who is able to do immeasurably more than all we ask or imagine, according to his power that is at work within us, to him be glory in the church and in Christ Jesus throughout all generations, for ever and ever! Amen."*

This passage can be divided into three main sections: Paul's posture in prayer (verses 14-15), the content of Paul's prayer (verses 16-19), and the doxology of praise (verses 20-21). Each section provides us with great insights into the nature of prayer, the power of God's love, and the glory of God.

Paul's posture in prayer (3:14-15)

Paul begins by describing his posture in prayer and his approach to God as Father.

Kneeling before the Father: "*For this reason I kneel before the Father.*" Paul's posture of kneeling indicates his deep reverence and humility before God. Kneeling is a physical expression of submission, worship, and dependence on God. It reflects Paul's recognition of God's sovereignty and his own need for divine intervention.

This posture of kneeling can inspire us to approach God with the same attitude of humility and reverence. It reminds us that prayer is not just a routine activity but a profound encounter with the Almighty God.

The Father of All: Paul addresses God as the Father "*... from whom every family in heaven and on earth derives its name.*" This emphasizes God's role as the Creator and Sustainer of all life. It highlights the universal fatherhood of God and the unity of all creation under His loving care. Recognizing God as our Father gives us a sense of belonging and identity. It assures us that we are part of His family and that He cares for us deeply.

The content of Paul's prayer (3:16-19)

Paul's prayer is rich with requests for spiritual strength, deeper understanding of Christ's love, and fullness in God.

I pray that out of his glorious riches he may strengthen you with power through his Spirit in your inner being." This strength is not physical but spiritual, affecting the inner being - the core of who we are.

The source of this strength is God's glorious riches, emphasizing His abundant and limitless resources. The Holy Spirit empowers us from within, enabling us to live out our faith with resilience and boldness.

Christ dwelling in our hearts: "So that Christ may dwell in your hearts through faith." This dwelling goes beyond a temporary visit; it signifies a permanent residence. Christ's presence in our hearts is foundational to our Christian life and growth. Faith is the means by which Christ dwells in us. It involves trusting in Him, relying on His promises, and allowing Him to shape our thoughts, desires, and actions.

Rooted and established in love: "And I pray that you, being rooted and established in love." Paul uses the metaphors of being rooted and established to describe the believers' foundation in love. Just as roots provide stability and nourishment to a plant, being rooted in love provides stability and growth in our spiritual lives.

Love is the soil in which our faith grows. It is the foundation of our relationship with God and with others. Being established in love means that love is the guiding principle and driving force of our lives.

Grasping the love of Christ: "May have power, together with all the Lord's holy people, to grasp how wide and long and high and deep is the love of Christ." Paul wants all believers to have the power to comprehend the vast dimensions of Christ's love.

This love is described as being wide, long, high, and deep, indicating it is immeasurable and boundless in its nature. Understanding the depth of Christ's love requires divine revelation and spiritual insight. It is a love that surpasses human understanding and is experienced in community with other believers.

Knowing the love that surpasses knowledge: "And to know this love that surpasses knowledge - that you may be filled to the measure of all the fullness of God." Paul prays for the believers to know the love of Christ that surpasses knowledge. This knowledge is not merely intellectual but experiential.

It involves a deep, personal encounter with the love of Christ. Being filled with the fullness of God means we are experiencing His presence and power in every aspect of our lives. It is the culmination of Paul's prayer, indicating a life that is fully saturated with God's love and grace.

The doxology of praise (3:20-21)

Paul concludes his prayer with a doxology of praise, acknowledging God's power and glory.

God's immeasurable power: "Now to him who is able to do immeasurably more than all we ask or imagine, according to his power that is at work within us." Paul praises God for His immeasurable power. God's ability to exceed our requests and imagination highlights His greatness and sovereignty.

His power is never limited by our own understanding or expectations. This power is at work within us through the Holy Spirit, enabling us to live out our faith and accomplish God's purposes. It assures us that God is actively involved in our lives and is able to do far more than we can comprehend.

Glory to God in the church and in Christ Jesus: "To him be glory in the church and in Christ Jesus throughout all generations, for ever and ever! Amen." Paul concludes with a declaration of glory to God. The church and Christ Jesus are the primary arenas where God's glory is displayed.

The church, as the body of Christ, reflects His glory through its unity, love, and mission. This declaration of glory spans all generations, indicating the eternal and unchanging nature of God's glory. It reminds us that our lives are part of a larger, eternal story that brings glory to God.

Practical Applications

Cultivate a posture of reverence in prayer. Emulate Paul's posture of kneeling in prayer. Approach God with humility, reverence, and dependence. Recognize that prayer is a sacred encounter with the Creator and Sustainer of all life.

Set aside dedicated times for prayer and create a space where you can kneel or sit quietly before God. Allow your physical posture to reflect the attitude of your heart as you seek God's presence and guidance. Experiment with different physical postures, such as kneeling, standing, or even lying flat on the floor, to express your reverence before God. You may even consider a prayer retreat where you can spend extended time in prayer and reflection. Use this time to deepen your relationship with God and to cultivate a posture of reverence in your prayer life.

Find a prayer partner or join a prayer group where you can pray together and encourage one another. Sharing your prayer experiences with others can help you grow in your understanding and practice of prayer.

Embrace your identity as God's child. Remember that you are a beloved child of God, part of His family. Let this identity shape your sense of belonging, purpose, and security. Trust in God's love and care for you. Reflect on Scriptures that affirm your identity as God's child, such as Romans 8:14-17 and 1 John 3:1-2. Meditate on these truths and let them sink deeply into your heart.

Surround yourself with a community of believers who can affirm and encourage your identity in Christ. Participate in small groups, Bible studies, and fellowship activities that foster a sense of belonging and support.

Pray for the Holy Spirit to strengthen you in your inner being. Recognize that true strength comes from God's glorious riches and the indwelling presence of the Holy Spirit.

Depend on His power to always sustain and empower you. Incorporate prayers for spiritual strength into your daily routine. Ask God to fill you with His Spirit and to empower you to live out your faith with resilience and boldness. Pray for strength in specific areas of your life where you feel weak or challenged. Study Scriptures that speak of God's strength and power, such as Isaiah 40:29-31 and Philippians 4:13. Reflect on these verses and allow them to strengthen and encourage you.

Invite Christ to dwell in your heart more fully through faith. Allow Him to shape your thoughts, desires, and actions. Trust in His presence and guidance.

Spend time in prayer and reflection, inviting Christ to be the centre of your life. Surrender your fears, worries, and desires to Him, and allow His love and peace to fill your heart. Keep a journal where you record your prayers and reflections on inviting Christ to dwell in your heart. Write down the ways you see Him working in your life and the changes you experience as you surrender to Him.

Engage in practices that help you grow in faith and trust in Christ. These may include regular Bible reading, prayer, worship, and fellowship with other believers. Allow these practices to strengthen your relationship with Christ.

Ground yourself in love. Cultivate a life that is rooted and established in love. Let love be the guiding principle and driving force in your relationships and actions. Seek to reflect Christ's love in all that you do.

Practice acts of love and kindness in your daily interactions. Look for opportunities to serve others and to demonstrate the love of Christ through your words and actions.

Reflect on how you can be a conduit of God's love to those around you. Participate in community service projects or volunteer opportunities that allow you to put your love into action.

Grasp the true depth of Christ's love. Pray for the power to comprehend the vast dimensions of Christ's love. Seek to understand and experience His love in deeper and more profound ways.

Recognize that this love surpasses human understanding. Engage in regular Bible study and meditation on passages that speak of Christ's love, such as Romans 8:35-39 and John 15:9-17. Reflect on these Scriptures and allow the Holy Spirit to reveal the depth of Christ's love to you.

Consider going on a spiritual retreat where you can focus on experiencing the love of Christ. Use this time to deepen your understanding and appreciation of His love.

Participate in small group discussions or Bible studies that focus on the theme of Christ's love. Share your insights and experiences with others and learn from their perspectives.

Experience the fullness of God. Seek to be filled with the fullness of God. Invite His presence and power to permeate every aspect of your life. Allow His love, grace, and truth to transform you from the inside out.

Spend time in worship and prayer, inviting God to fill you with His presence. Seek to align your life with His will and to live in a way that reflects His character and glory.

Make worship a regular part of your daily routine. Practice spiritual disciplines that help you grow in your experience of God's fullness. These may include fasting, meditation, and silence. Seek to cultivate a deeper relationship with God through these disciplines.

Spend time reflecting on what it means to be filled with the fullness of God. Consider how you can invite His presence and power to permeate every aspect of your life. Write down your reflections and seek to live out these truths.

Living Ephesians 3:14-21 in daily life

To fully internalize and live out the truths of Ephesians 3:14-21, we must integrate these principles into our daily lives. Here are some practical ways to do that:

Daily Reminders of God's Love: Start each day by reminding yourself of God's love and presence in your life. This could be through a morning devotion, prayer, or reading Scripture. Let the truth of God's love shape your mindset and actions throughout the day.

Practicing Gratitude: Cultivate a habit of gratitude by regularly thanking God for His love and the new life you have in Christ. Keep a gratitude journal where you write down specific ways God has blessed you.

Extending Love to Others: Make a conscious effort to extend love to others in your interactions. This means being patient, forgiving, and kind, even when it's difficult. Let the love you have received from God overflow into your relationships.

Seeking God's Guidance: Regularly seek God's guidance in discovering and walking in the good works He has prepared for you.

Pray for clarity, wisdom, and opportunities to serve. Be open to where God leads you and be willing to step out in faith.

Building Community: Surround yourself with a community of believers who can encourage and support you in your walk with Christ. Participate in small groups, Bible studies, and church activities that foster spiritual growth and accountability.

Reflecting on Your Testimony: Reflect regularly on your testimony and the ways God has transformed your life. Share your story with others as a way to encourage and inspire them. Let your life be a living testimony of God's love.

Conclusion

In Ephesians 3:14-21, Paul prays for the believers to be strengthened with power, to grasp the depth of Christ's love, and to be filled with the fullness of God. His prayer reveals the profound nature of our relationship with God and the transformative power of His love.

As we reflect on these truths, let us more fully embrace our identity as God's children, seeking spiritual strength, invite Christ to dwell more fully in our hearts, as we root ourselves in love, grasping the depth of Christ's love, and experience the fullness of God.

May we carry these truths in our hearts and live out our faith boldly and joyfully. It is my prayer that we would all continue to grow in our understanding of God's love and live out the truths of this powerful prayer with confidence and grace.

8. WORTHY OF OUR CALLING

As we continue our exploration of the book of Ephesians, we now examine a passage that calls us to live a life worthy of our calling. In the opening verses of chapter four, Paul shifts from the theological foundations he has laid in the previous chapters to some practical instructions for living out our faith. This passage emphasizes unity, maturity and growth within the body of Christ.

> **Ephesians 4:1-16** *"As a prisoner for the Lord, then, I urge you to live a life worthy of the calling you have received. Be completely humble and gentle; be patient, bearing with one another in love.*
>
> *Make every effort to keep the unity of the Spirit through the bond of peace. There is one body and one Spirit, just as you were called to one hope when you were called; one Lord, one faith, one baptism; one God and Father of all, who is over all and through all and in all.*
>
> *But to each one of us grace has been given as Christ apportioned it. This is why it says: 'When he ascended on high, he took many captives and gave gifts to his people.' (What does 'he ascended' mean except that he also descended to the lower, earthly regions? He who descended is the very one who ascended higher than all the heavens, in order to fill the whole universe.)*
>
> *So Christ himself gave the apostles, the prophets, the evangelists, the pastors and teachers, to equip his people for works of service, so that the body of Christ may be built up until we all reach unity in the faith and in the knowledge of the Son of God and become mature, attaining to the whole measure of the fullness of Christ.*

Then we will no longer be infants, tossed back and forth by the waves, and blown here and there by every wind of teaching and by the cunning and craftiness of people in their deceitful scheming. Instead, speaking the truth in love, we will grow to become in every respect the mature body of him who is the head, that is, Christ. From him the whole body, joined and held together by every supporting ligament, grows and builds itself up in love, as each part does its work."

This passage can be divided into three main sections: the call to unity (verses 1-6), the diversity of gifts (verses 7-12), and the goal of maturity (verses 13-16). Each section provides us with profound insights into how we are to live out our calling as followers of Christ.

The call to unity (4:1-6)

Paul begins by urging the believers to live a life worthy of their calling, emphasizing the importance of unity within the body of Christ.

Living worthy of your calling: "As a prisoner for the Lord, then, I urge you to live a life worthy of the calling you have received." Paul, writing from prison, urges the believers to live a life that reflects the calling they have received. This calling refers to their identity and purpose as followers of Christ.

Living worthy of this calling involves aligning our lives with the values and principles of the gospel. Reflect on your own calling as a follower of Christ. Consider how you can live in a way that honours and reflects this calling. Ask God to help you align your thoughts, actions, and attitudes with His will.

Characteristics of unity: "Be completely humble and gentle; be patient, bearing with one another in love." Paul lists several characteristics that are essential for maintaining unity within the body of Christ: humility, gentleness, patience, and love. These virtues create an environment where unity can thrive and relationships can be strengthened. Strive to cultivate these virtues in your interactions with others. Practice humility by putting others' needs before your own, gentleness by responding with kindness, patience by being slow to anger, and love by seeking the best for others.

Keeping the unity of the Spirit: "Make every effort to keep the unity of the Spirit through the bond of peace." Paul emphasizes the importance of actively maintaining the unity of the Spirit. This unity is not something we create but something we are called to preserve. It is a gift from the Holy Spirit, and it is our responsibility to protect and nurture it. We must make a conscious effort to promote peace and unity within our church and community. We should be intentional about resolving conflicts, fostering understanding, and building relationships based on mutual respect and love.

The basis of unity: "There is one body and one Spirit, just as you were called to one hope when you were called; one Lord, one faith, one baptism; one God and Father of all, who is over all and through all and in all." Paul highlights the theological basis for unity: there is one body, one Spirit, one hope, one Lord, one faith, one baptism, and one God and Father of all.

These shared beliefs and experiences unite us as followers of Christ. So reflect on the unity we have in Christ. Celebrate the shared beliefs and experiences that bind us together as one body. Let these truths strengthen your commitment to promoting unity and peace within the church.

The diversity of gifts (4:7-12)

Paul transitions now to discussing the diversity of gifts within the body of Christ, emphasizing that each believer has been given grace according to Christ's apportionment.

Grace given to each believer: "But to each one of us grace has been given as Christ apportioned it." Paul acknowledges that each believer has been given grace according to the measure of Christ's gift. This grace refers to the spiritual gifts and abilities that Christ has bestowed upon His followers. Recognize that you have been given gifts and abilities in Christ. Reflect on how you can use these gifts to serve others and contribute to the growth and unity of the body of Christ.

The ascension and descent of Christ: "This is why it says: 'When he ascended on high, he took many captives and gave gifts to his people.' (What does 'he ascended' mean except that he also descended to the lower, earthly regions? He who descended is the very one who ascended higher than all the heavens, in order to fill the whole universe.)" Paul refers to Christ's ascension and descent to emphasize His authority to bestow gifts.

Christ's descent to the lower regions likely refers to His incarnation and His victory over sin and death. His ascension signifies His exaltation and His authority over all things. Reflect on the significance of Christ's descent and ascension. Consider how His victory and authority impact your life and your calling as a follower of Christ.

Gifts for equipping the Church: "So Christ himself gave the apostles, the prophets, the evangelists, the pastors and teachers, to equip his people for works of service, so that the body of Christ may be built up."

Paul lists specific leadership gifts that Christ has given to the church: apostles, prophets, evangelists, pastors, and teachers. These gifts are given to equip the believers for works of service and to build up the body of Christ. Reflect on the role of these leadership gifts within the church. Consider how you can support and encourage those who serve in these roles. Recognize the importance of being equipped for service and seek opportunities to grow and serve within the body of Christ.

The goal of maturity (4:13-16)

Paul concludes this section by emphasizing the goal of maturity and growth within the body of Christ.

Unity in faith and knowledge: "*Until we all reach unity in the faith and in the knowledge of the Son of God and become mature, attaining to the whole measure of the fullness of Christ.*" Paul highlights the goal of unity in faith and knowledge of the Son of God. This unity leads to maturity and the fullness of Christ. Maturity involves growing in our understanding of Christ and becoming more like Him by submitting more to His life within us. Reflect on your own spiritual growth and maturity. Consider how you can deepen your faith and knowledge of Christ. Seek opportunities for spiritual growth, such as Bible studies, discipleship, and personal reflection.

Stability in doctrine: "*Then we will no longer be infants, tossed back and forth by the waves, and blown here and there by every wind of teaching and by the cunning and craftiness of people in their deceitful scheming.*" Paul emphasizes the importance of stability in doctrine. Maturity involves being grounded in sound teaching and not being swayed by false doctrines or deceptive teachings. So you should commit to studying and understanding sound doctrine.

Seek guidance from trusted teachers and mentors and be discerning about the teachings you encounter. Ground yourself in the truth of God's Word.

Speaking the truth in love: "Instead, speaking the truth in love, we will grow to become in every respect the mature body of him who is the head, that is, Christ." Paul highlights the importance of speaking the truth in love. This balance of truth and love is essential for growth and maturity. It involves being honest and forthright while also being compassionate and caring. Practice speaking the truth in love in your interactions with others. Seek to build up and encourage others through your words. Strive to balance honesty with compassion and seek to reflect Christ in your communication.

Growth and building up in love: "From him the whole body, joined and held together by every supporting ligament, grows and builds itself up in love, as each part does its work." Paul concludes by emphasizing the interconnectedness and the essential interdependence of the body of Christ. Growth and maturity occur as each part does its work and the body builds itself up in love. Reflect on your role within the body of Christ. Consider how you can contribute to the growth and building up of the church. Recognize the importance of working together and supporting one another in love.

Practical Applications

Live a life worthy of your calling. Reflect on your calling as a follower of Christ and consider how you can live in a way that honours and reflects this calling. Ask God to help you align your thoughts, actions, and attitudes with His will. Make a daily commitment to live out your calling with integrity and purpose.

Seek to honour God in all that you do and to be a reflection of His love and grace to those around you. As you spend time reflecting on your calling as a follower of Christ, consider how you can live in a way that honours and reflects this calling. Write down specific actions and attitudes you want to cultivate in your life. Find an accountability partner who can support and encourage you in living out your calling. Share your goals and commitments with them and seek their guidance and accountability.

Incorporate daily devotions and reflections into your routine. Use these times to realign your heart and mind with God's will and to seek His guidance for living out your calling.

Cultivate Unity within the Body of Christ. Strive to promote unity and peace within your church and community. Practice humility, gentleness, patience, and love in your interactions with others.

Be intentional about resolving conflicts and building relationships based on mutual respect and understanding. Participate in church activities and initiatives that promote unity and inclusivity. Look for opportunities to build bridges and foster understanding among diverse groups of people.

Practice healthy conflict resolution in your relationships. When conflicts arise, seek to address them with grace, humility, and a desire for reconciliation. Use biblical principles of peacemaking, such as those found in Matthew 18:15-17 and Romans 12:18. Engage with your church community and participate in activities that promote unity and inclusivity.

Look for opportunities to build relationships with people from diverse backgrounds and experiences. Demonstrate your commitment to unity through acts of service. Look for ways to serve others within your church and community and seek to build bridges through your actions.

Recognize and use your Spiritual gifts. Reflect on the unique gifts and abilities that Christ has given the church through you. Consider how you can use these gifts to serve others and contribute to the growth and unity of the body of Christ. Seek opportunities to develop and use those gifts within the church and community.

Be open to feedback and guidance from others and be willing to step out in faith to serve and make a difference. Take a spiritual gifts assessment to help identify your unique gifts and abilities. Reflect on how you can use those gifts to serve others and contribute to the growth of the body of Christ.

Seek out service opportunities within your church and community that align with your gifts and passions. Be open to trying new things and stepping out of your comfort zone to serve. Find a mentor who can help you develop and use your spiritual gifts. Seek their guidance and support as you grow in your understanding and application of your gifts.

Support and encourage Church leaders. Recognize the important role of evangelists, pastors, and teachers within the church. Support and encourage those who serve in these roles and seek to be equipped for service through their guidance and teaching. Pray for your church leaders and offer your support and encouragement. Be proactive in seeking out opportunities for growth and service and be willing to invest in the development of others.

Commit to regularly praying for your church leaders. Pray for their wisdom, strength, and guidance as they serve and lead the church. Offer words of encouragement and support to your church leaders. Let them know that you appreciate their service and leadership. Be an active participant in your church's ministries and initiatives. Offer your time, talents, and resources to support the work of your church and its leaders.

Pursue spiritual maturity: Commit to growing in your faith and knowledge of Christ. Seek opportunities for spiritual growth, such as Bible studies, discipleship, and personal reflection. Be grounded in sound doctrine and discerning about the teachings you encounter. Make spiritual growth a priority in your life. Set aside regular time for Bible study, prayer, and reflection. Seek out mentors and accountability partners who can help you grow in your faith.

Join a Bible study group focused on deepening your understanding of Scripture. Study books of the Bible, specific topics, or themes that help you grow in your faith. Seek out discipleship relationships where you can learn from more mature believers and mentor others who are newer in their faith. These relationships can provide valuable support and encouragement in your spiritual growth. Spend regular time in personal reflection and journaling. Reflect on your spiritual journey, the areas where you need to grow, and the ways God is working in your life.

Speak the truth in love. Practice speaking the truth in love in your interactions with others. Seek to build up and encourage others through your words. Strive to balance honesty with compassion and seek to reflect Christ in your communication. Be intentional about your words and how they impact others.

Seek to build others up and to encourage them in their faith journey. Be willing to have difficult conversations with grace and compassion.

Work on developing effective communication skills that balance truth and love. Practice active listening, empathy, and compassionate responses in your interactions with others. Make a habit of offering encouragement and affirmation to others. Look for opportunities to build others up and to speak life-giving words into their lives. When offering constructive feedback or addressing difficult issues, do so with grace and compassion. Seek to build others up and to promote growth and healing through your words.

Conclusion

In Ephesians 4:1-16, Paul calls us to live a life worthy of our calling, emphasizing unity, maturity, and growth within the body of Christ. As we reflect on these truths, let us strive to live out our calling with integrity and purpose, promote unity and peace, use our spiritual gifts to serve others, support and encourage our church leaders, pursue spiritual maturity, and speak the truth in love.

9. OLD SELF, NEW SELF

As our study of Ephesians progresses, we come now to a passage that challenges us to live transformed lives. In the second half of Ephesians 4, Paul instructs us to put off the old self and to put on the new self, emphasizing the importance of living in righteousness and holiness.

This passage provides practical guidance on how to live out our new identity in Christ.

> **Ephesians 4:17-32** *"So I tell you this, and insist on it in the Lord, that you must no longer live as the Gentiles do, in the futility of their thinking. They are darkened in their understanding and separated from the life of God because of the ignorance that is in them due to the hardening of their hearts. Having lost all sensitivity, they have given themselves over to sensuality so as to indulge in every kind of impurity, and they are full of greed.*
>
> *That, however, is not the way of life you learned when you heard about Christ and were taught in him in accordance with the truth that is in Jesus. You were taught, with regard to your former way of life, to put off your old self, which is being corrupted by its deceitful desires; to be made new in the attitude of your minds; and to put on the new self, created to be like God in true righteousness and holiness.*
>
> *Therefore, each of you must put off falsehood and speak truthfully to your neighbour, for we are all members of one body. 'In your anger do not sin': Do not let the sun go down while you are still angry, and do not give the devil a foothold. Anyone who has been stealing must steal no longer, but must work, doing something useful with their own hands, that they may have something to share with those in need.*

Do not let any unwholesome talk come out of your mouths, but only what is helpful for building others up according to their needs, that it may benefit those who listen. And do not grieve the Holy Spirit of God, with whom you were sealed for the day of redemption. Get rid of all bitterness, rage and anger, brawling and slander, along with every form of malice. Be kind and compassionate to one another, forgiving each other, just as in Christ God forgave you."

This passage can be divided into three main sections: the contrast between the old self and the new self (verses 17-24), practical instructions for living out the new self (verses 25-29), and the call to kindness, compassion, and forgiveness (verses 30-32). Each section provides us with considerable insight into how we are to live transformed lives in Christ.

The old self vs. the new self (4:17-24)

Paul begins by emphasizing the stark contrast between the old self and the new self. He urges the believers to no longer live as the Gentiles do but to embrace their new identity in Christ.

The futility of the Gentiles' thinking ...

"So I tell you this, and insist on it in the Lord, that you must no longer live as the Gentiles do, in the futility of their thinking." Paul insists that the believers must no longer live like the Gentiles, whose thinking is characterized by futility. This futility refers to their aimless and meaningless way of life, driven by worldly desires and pursuits.

Reflect on the ways in which worldly thinking and values may be influencing your life. Ask God to help you identify and remove any areas of futility in your thinking.

Darkened understanding and separation from God ...

"They are darkened in their understanding and separated from the life of God because of the ignorance that is in them due to the hardening of their hearts." The Gentiles' understanding is darkened, and they are separated from the life of God due to their ignorance and hardening of hearts.

This separation leads to a life of spiritual blindness and estrangement from God. Consider how ignorance and hardness of heart can impact your relationship with God. Seek to cultivate a soft and receptive heart, open to God's truth and guidance.

Giving themselves over to sensuality ...

"Having lost all sensitivity, they have given themselves over to sensuality so as to indulge in every kind of impurity, and they are full of greed." The Gentiles have lost all sensitivity to moral and spiritual matters, giving themselves over to sensuality and indulging in impurity and greed.

This lifestyle is marked by a lack of self-control and a pursuit of selfish desires. Reflect on any areas of your life where you may be tempted to indulge in impurity or greed. Ask God to help you develop self-control and to live in a way that honours Him.

Learning the way of Christ ...

"That, however, is not the way of life you learned when you heard about Christ and were taught in him in accordance with the truth that is in Jesus." Paul contrasts the Gentiles' way of life with the way of life the believers have learned in Christ. The truth that is in Jesus calls for a radically different way of living.

Reflect on the teachings of Christ and how they challenge and transform your way of life. Commit to learning and living out the truth that is in Jesus.

Putting off the old self ...

"You were taught, with regard to your former way of life, to put off your old self, which is being corrupted by its deceitful desires." The believers are taught to put off their old self, which is characterized by deceitful desires and corruption. This involves a conscious and deliberate rejection of the old way of life. Consider what it means to put off your old self. Reflect on the specific attitudes, behaviours, and desires that you need to let go of in order to live a transformed life in Christ.

Being made new in the attitude of your minds ...

"To be made new in the attitude of your minds." Paul is emphasizing the importance of renewing the mind. This renewal involves a transformation in the way we think, aligning our thoughts with God's truth and perspective. Commit to renewing your mind through regular study and meditation on God's Word. Allow His truth to shape and transform your thoughts and attitudes.

Putting on the new self ...

"And to put on the new self, created to be like God in true righteousness and holiness." The believers are called to put on the new self, which is created to be like God in true righteousness and holiness. This new self reflects the character and nature of God. Reflect on what it means to put on the new self. Consider how you can cultivate righteousness and holiness in your daily life.

Living out the new self (4:25-29)

Paul provides practical instructions for how to live out the new self, emphasizing honesty, self-control, generosity, and wholesome speech.

Speaking truthfully ...

"Therefore, each of you must put off falsehood and speak truthfully to your neighbour, for we are all members of one body." Paul instructs the believers to put off falsehood and to speak truthfully to one another. Honesty is really essential for maintaining trust and unity within the body of Christ.

Commit to speaking truthfully in your interactions with others. Reflect on the importance of honesty and integrity in your relationships.

Handling anger appropriately ...

"'In your anger do not sin': Do not let the sun go down while you are still angry, and do not give the devil a foothold." Paul acknowledges that anger is a natural emotion but cautions against letting it lead to sin. He advises the believers to resolve their anger quickly and not to let it fester.

Reflect on how you handle anger. Seek to address conflicts and resolve anger in a healthy and timely manner. Avoid giving the devil a foothold through unresolved anger.

Working and sharing ...

"Anyone who has been stealing must steal no longer, but must work, doing something useful with their own hands, that they may have something to share with those in need."

Paul encourages the believers to engage in honest work and to use their resources to help those in need. This reflects a life of integrity and generosity. Consider how you can use your skills and resources to benefit others. Commit to working diligently and sharing generously with those in need.

Wholesome speech ...

"Do not let any unwholesome talk come out of your mouths, but only what is helpful for building others up according to their needs, that it may benefit those who listen." Paul instructs the believers to avoid unwholesome talk and to speak in a way that builds others up. Wholesome speech reflects a transformed heart and mind.

Reflect on the words that you speak. Commit to using your speech to encourage and build up others. Avoid gossip, negativity, and harmful language.

Kindness, compassion, and forgiveness (4:30-32)

Paul concludes this section by calling the believers to exhibit kindness, compassion, and forgiveness, reflecting the character of Christ.

Do not grieve the Holy Spirit ...

"And do not grieve the Holy Spirit of God, with whom you were sealed for the day of redemption." Paul warns against grieving the Holy Spirit. Our actions and attitudes can either please or grieve the Holy Spirit who dwells within us.

Reflect on how your actions and attitudes impact the Holy Spirit. Seek to live in a way that honours and pleases Him.

Getting rid of negative behaviours ...

"Get rid of all bitterness, rage and anger, brawling and slander, along with every form of malice." Paul lists several negative behaviours that the believers are to get rid of: bitterness, rage, anger, brawling, slander, and malice.

These behaviours are contrary to the new self and must be put away. Reflect on any negative behaviours or attitudes that you need to let go of. Ask God to help you remove these from your life and to replace them with positive, Christ-like qualities.

Being kind and compassionate ...

"Be kind and compassionate to one another." Paul calls the believers to be kind and compassionate. Kindness and compassion reflect the heart of Christ and build strong, loving relationships within the body of Christ.

Commit to showing kindness and compassion in your interactions with others. Look for opportunities to extend grace, understanding, and support to those around you.

Forgiving each other ...

"Forgiving each other, just as in Christ God forgave you." Paul emphasizes the importance of forgiveness, reminding the believers of the forgiveness they have received in Christ. Forgiveness is essential for healing and maintaining healthy relationships.

Reflect on any areas where you need to extend or seek forgiveness. Make a fresh commitment to always practice forgiveness, remembering the grace and forgiveness you have received from God.

Practical Applications

Renew your mind: Join a Bible study group or follow a personal reading plan that helps you grow in your understanding of Scripture. Seek to apply what you learn to your daily life. Choose specific books of the Bible or topics to explore in depth. Seek God's wisdom and revelation as you study.

Memorize key Scriptures that speak to the renewal of the mind. Let these verses encourage and strengthen you, especially during times of difficulty or doubt. Set aside time for spiritual retreats or quiet days where you can focus on prayer, reflection, and seeking God's presence. These times of intentional solitude can provide space for God to speak and reveal His will.

Cultivate honesty and integrity: Commit to always speak truthfully in all your interactions. Reflect on the importance of honesty and integrity in your relationships. Avoid falsehood and seek to build trust through truthful communication. Be willing to admit mistakes and seek to build relationships based on trust and mutual respect.

Find an accountability partner who can support and encourage you in your commitment to honesty and integrity. Share your goals and commitments with them and seek their guidance and accountability. Seek to live in a way that honours God and reflects His truth.

Handle anger in a healthy way: Reflect on how you handle anger and seek to address conflicts in a healthy and timely manner. Avoid letting anger fester and giving the devil a foothold. Practice forgiveness and seek reconciliation in your relationships.

Develop healthy strategies for managing anger, such as taking a break to cool down, seeking counsel from trusted friends, and praying for guidance and wisdom.

Practice healthy conflict resolution in your relationships. When conflicts arise, seek to address them with grace, humility, and a desire for reconciliation. Reflect on the importance of forgiveness and seek to practice it in your relationships. Remember the grace and forgiveness you have received from God and extend it to others.

Engage in honest work and generosity: Use your skills and resources to benefit others. Commit to working diligently and sharing generously with those in need. Reflect on how you can use your work and resources to make a positive impact on your community. Look for opportunities to volunteer and serve those in need. Consider how you can use your time, talents, and resources to support charitable organizations and initiatives. Practice generosity in your daily life. Look for ways to share your resources and support those in need.

Use wholesome speech: Reflect on the words you speak and commit to using your speech to encourage and build up others. Avoid gossip, negativity, and harmful language. Seek to speak in a way that reflects a transformed heart and mind. Practice speaking words of encouragement, affirmation, and support to those around you. Be intentional about using your words to uplift and edify.

Reflect on the words you speak and seek to use positive communication in your interactions with others. Avoid gossip, negativity, and harmful language. Practice active listening in your conversations. Seek to understand and empathize with others and respond with kindness and compassion.

Exhibit kindness, compassion, and forgiveness: Commit to showing kindness and compassion in your interactions with others. Always look for opportunities to extend grace, understanding, and support to those around you. Practice forgiveness, remembering the grace and forgiveness you have received from God. Reflect on the character of Christ and seek to emulate His kindness, His compassion, and forgiveness in your daily life. Look for opportunities to show kindness and compassion in your daily interactions. Reflect on how you can be a conduit of God's love to those around you.

Conclusion

In Ephesians 4:17-32, Paul challenges us to put off the old self and to put on the new self, emphasizing the importance of living in righteousness and holiness. As we reflect on these truths, let us strive to live transformed lives that reflect our new identity in Christ. May we cultivate honesty and integrity, manage anger healthily, engage in honest work and generosity, use wholesome speech, and exhibit kindness, compassion, and forgiveness.

10. CHILDREN OF LIGHT

In the first part of Ephesians 5, Paul exhorts us to imitate God, walk in love, and live as light in a dark world. This passage provides practical guidance on how to reflect the character of Christ in our daily lives, emphasizing purity, wisdom, and thanksgiving.

> **Ephesians 5:1-20** *"Follow God's example, therefore, as dearly loved children and walk in the way of love, just as Christ loved us and gave himself up for us as a fragrant offering and sacrifice to God. But among you there must not be even a hint of sexual immorality, or of any kind of impurity, or of greed, because these are improper for God's holy people.*
>
> *Nor should there be obscenity, foolish talk or coarse joking, which are out of place, but rather thanksgiving. For of this you can be sure: No immoral, impure or greedy person - such a person is an idolater - has any inheritance in the kingdom of Christ and of God. Let no one deceive you with empty words, for because of such things God's wrath comes on those who are disobedient.*
>
> *Therefore, do not be partners with them. For you were once darkness, but now you are light in the Lord. Live as children of light (for the fruit of the light consists in all goodness, righteousness and truth) and find out what pleases the Lord.*
>
> *Have nothing to do with the fruitless deeds of darkness, but rather expose them. It is shameful even to mention what the disobedient do in secret. But everything exposed by the light becomes visible - and everything that is illuminated becomes a light. This is why it is said: 'Wake up, sleeper, rise from the dead, and Christ will shine on you.'*

Be very careful, then, how you live - not as unwise but as wise, making the most of every opportunity, because the days are evil. Therefore, do not be foolish, but understand what the Lord's will is. Do not get drunk on wine, which leads to debauchery. Instead, be filled with the Spirit, speaking to one another with psalms, hymns, and songs from the Spirit. Sing and make music from your heart to the Lord, always giving thanks to God the Father for everything, in the name of our Lord Jesus Christ."

This passage can be divided into three main sections: the call to imitate God and walk in love (verses 1-7), the exhortation to live as children of light (verses 8-14), and the instruction to walk in wisdom and be filled with the Spirit (verses 15-20). Each section provides us with practical guidance on how to live out our faith in a way that reflects the character of Christ.

The call to follow God's example (5:1-7)

Paul begins this passage with a powerful exhortation: *"Follow God's example, therefore, as dearly loved children and walk in the way of love, just as Christ loved us and gave himself up for us as a fragrant offering and sacrifice to God."*

This call to follow God's example is rooted in our identity as His dearly loved children. Just as children naturally seek to imitate their parents, we are called to imitate our heavenly Father.

Reflecting God's values involves walking in love and following the example of Christ. Paul reminds us that Christ loved us and gave Himself up for us as a fragrant offering and sacrifice to God. This selfless, sacrificial love is the standard for our conduct. We are called to love others with the same kind of love that Christ has shown us.

Paul then contrasts this call to love with a list of behaviours that are incompatible with our new identity in Christ: *"But among you there must not be even a hint of sexual immorality, or of any kind of impurity, or of greed, because these are improper for God's holy people. Nor should there be obscenity, foolish talk or coarse joking, which are out of place, but rather thanksgiving."*

Sexual immorality, impurity, and greed are behaviours that belong to the old self and have no place in the life of a believer. These behaviours are characterized by selfishness and a disregard for God's standards. Paul emphasizes that such behaviours must not even be named among us, highlighting the importance of maintaining purity and integrity.

In addition to avoiding immoral behaviours, Paul also warns against obscenity, foolish talk, and coarse joking. These forms of speech are inappropriate for believers and can undermine our witness. Instead, we are called to cultivate a spirit of thanksgiving, reflecting an attitude of gratitude and praise.

Paul provides a solemn warning about the consequences of engaging in such behaviours: *"For of this you can be sure: No immoral, impure or greedy person - such a person is an idolater - has any inheritance in the kingdom of Christ and of God. Let no one deceive you with empty words, for because of such things God's wrath comes on those who are disobedient."*

Those who persist in these sinful behaviours without repentance demonstrate that they have not experienced the transforming power of God's grace. Paul warns against being deceived by empty words that minimize the seriousness of sin. The wrath of God is a real consequence for those who continue in disobedience.

Therefore, Paul exhorts us: "*Therefore do not be partners with them.*" We are called to separate ourselves from the practices and influences of those who live in disobedience. This separation does not mean avoiding all contact with unbelievers but rather refusing to participate in their sinful behaviours and values.

The exhortation to live as children of light (5:8-14)

Paul continues with an exhortation to live as children of light: "*For you were once darkness, but now you are light in the Lord. Live as children of light (for the fruit of the light consists in all goodness, righteousness and truth) and find out what pleases the Lord.*"

Paul reminds us of our former condition: "*For you were once darkness.*" This description emphasizes the totality of our previous state of sin and separation from God. However, through Christ, we have been transformed: "but now you are light in the Lord." This new identity as light reflects our relationship with Christ, who is the Light of the world.

As children of light, we are called to walk in a manner that reflects our new identity. Paul describes the fruit of light as consisting of all goodness, righteousness, and truth. These qualities are the evidence of a life transformed by the light of Christ. We are called to pursue what is pleasing to the Lord, seeking to align our lives with His will.

Paul then instructs us to "*Have nothing to do with the fruitless deeds of darkness, but rather expose them. It is shameful even to mention what the disobedient do in secret. But everything exposed by the light becomes visible - and everything that is illuminated becomes a light. This is why it is said: 'Wake up, sleeper, rise from the dead, and Christ will shine on you.'*"

We are called to reject the fruitless deeds of darkness and to expose them. This involves not only avoiding participation in sinful behaviours but also shining the light of truth on them. Exposing darkness means bringing sin into the light of God's truth, leading to conviction and transformation.

Paul acknowledges that it is shameful even to mention what the disobedient do in secret. This therefore highlights the pervasiveness of sin and the need for vigilance in guarding our hearts and minds.

However, when sin is exposed by the light, it becomes visible, and everything that is illuminated becomes a light. This transformative power of light brings hope and renewal.

Paul concludes this section with a call to awaken: *"Wake up, sleeper, rise from the dead, and Christ will shine on you."* This call to awaken is a summons to spiritual vigilance and renewal. It is a reminder that Christ's light brings life and transformation to those who respond to His call.

Walk in wisdom, filled with the Spirit (5:15-20)

Paul then shifts to a focus on wisdom and being filled with the Spirit: *"Be very careful, then, how you live - not as unwise but as wise, making the most of every opportunity, because the days are evil. Therefore, do not be foolish, but understand what the Lord's will is."*

Paul calls us to walk with wisdom, being careful and intentional in how we live. This involves making the most of every opportunity, recognizing that the days are evil. The urgency of the times calls for discernment and purposeful living. We are to seek God's will and align our lives with His purposes.

Paul contrasts wisdom with foolishness, urging us to avoid foolishness and to seek understanding of the Lord's will. This understanding comes through a deep relationship with God, rooted in His Word and guided by the Holy Spirit. Wisdom involves applying God's truth to our daily lives, making decisions that reflect His character and values.

Paul then gives a specific instruction: "*Do not get drunk on wine, which leads to debauchery. Instead, be filled with the Spirit.*" This instruction highlights the contrast between worldly indulgence and spiritual fullness.

Drunkenness leads to debauchery, a lifestyle of excess and moral corruption. In contrast, being filled with the Spirit leads to a life that is controlled and guided by God's presence.

To be filled with the Spirit means to be under the influence and control of the Holy Spirit. This involves a continual surrender to His leading and a dependence on His power. Being filled with the Spirit results in a life marked by joy, thanksgiving, and mutual encouragement.

Paul describes the characteristics of a Spirit-filled life: "*speaking to one another with psalms, hymns, and songs from the Spirit. Sing and make music from your heart to the Lord, always giving thanks to God the Father for everything, in the name of our Lord Jesus Christ.*"

A Spirit-filled life is characterized by worship and praise. This involves speaking to one another with psalms, hymns, and songs from the Spirit, encouraging and edifying each other through worship. Singing and making music from our hearts to the Lord reflects a deep, inner joy that overflows in worship.

Thanksgiving is another hallmark of a Spirit-filled life. We are called to give thanks always and for everything, recognizing God's sovereignty and goodness in all circumstances. This attitude of gratitude is rooted in our relationship with God and reflects a trust in His providence.

Practical Applications

Radiate God's love: Reflect on the sacrificial love of Christ and seek to imitate it in your daily interactions. Consider ways to demonstrate selfless love to those around you, especially in challenging situations. Ask God to help you love others with the same kind of love that Christ has shown you.

Take time to examine your relationships and identify areas where you can grow in love. Are there people in your life who are difficult to love? Ask God to soften your heart and to give you the grace to love them as He does. Begin by identifying small, everyday opportunities to show kindness and love to those around you. This could be as simple as offering a listening ear to a friend, helping a neighbour with groceries, or showing patience in a difficult situation. Acts of kindness are a tangible way to reflect Christ's love.

Reflect on any unresolved conflicts or grudges you may be holding. Ask God for the strength and grace to forgive those who have wronged you, just as Christ has forgiven you. Seek reconciliation where possible, fostering peace and unity in your relationships. Look for ways to go above and beyond in demonstrating love. This could mean sacrificing your time, resources, or comfort to meet the needs of others. Consider volunteering for a local charity, supporting a family in need, or dedicating time to mentor someone in your community.

Cultivate purity and integrity: Avoid behaviours and speech that are incompatible with your identity in Christ. Commit to living a life of purity and integrity, both in your actions and in your words. Seek to honour God in all areas of your life. Reflect on your daily habits and interactions. Are there areas where you need to make changes to align with God's heart? Ask God to help you cultivate purity and integrity in every area of your life.

Find a trusted friend or mentor with whom you can share your struggles and goals for purity and integrity. Accountability partnerships can help to provide support, encouragement and prayer as you seek to live a life that honours God. Be mindful of the media, conversations, and environments you engage with. Choose to consume content that aligns with your values and uplifts your spirit. Create boundaries that help you avoid situations that may lead to temptation or compromise your integrity.

Spend time each day reading and meditating on God's Word. Allow His truth to renew your mind and strengthen your resolve to live a life of purity and integrity. Use a journal to record your reflections and prayers, seeking God's guidance and strength.

Live as children of light: Embrace your identity as light in the Lord and seek to reflect His character in all that you do. Pursue what is good, right, and true, and seek to discern what is pleasing to the Lord. Be intentional about living in a way that reflects your new identity in Christ.

Consider practical ways to shine the light of Christ in your community. Are there opportunities to serve and to share the love of Christ with others? Ask God to guide you in being a light in the darkness.

Get involved in community service or outreach programs. Use your gifts and talents to make a positive impact and to share the love of Christ with others. Look for opportunities to serve in your church, local shelters, or community centres. Be intentional about sharing your faith with others. Look for opportunities to have conversations about Jesus and to share your testimony.

Be prepared to give a reason for the hope that you have and do so with gentleness and respect. Strive to be a positive influence in your workplace, school, or social circles. Let your actions and words reflect the character of Christ, demonstrating integrity, kindness, and compassion in all that you do.

Expose and reject darkness: Be vigilant in rejecting the fruitless deeds of darkness and exposing them with the light of God's truth. This involves being aware of the influences and values of the world and choosing to live according to God's standards. Reflect on the areas of your life where you may be influenced by darkness. Are there habits or behaviours that need to be addressed?

Ask God to help you expose and reject darkness, living in the light of His truth. Stay informed about the cultural and societal issues that may impact your faith. Use discernment to identify areas where the values of the world conflict with God's standards. Pray for wisdom to navigate these challenges and to stand firm in your convictions.

Set some boundaries that help you avoid compromising situations. This may involve limiting your exposure to certain media, avoiding specific social settings, or being cautious about the company you keep. Seek God's guidance in establishing and maintaining these boundaries. Be courageous in speaking the truth in love.

When you encounter sin or injustice, address it with grace and humility. Use your voice to advocate for what is right and to shine the light of Christ in dark places.

Walk in wisdom: Seek to live with wisdom, making the most of every opportunity and understanding the will of the Lord. Be intentional and purposeful in your daily decisions, aligning them with God's purposes. Reflect on how you can grow in wisdom. Are there areas where you need to seek God's guidance and understanding?

Evaluate how you spend your time and make adjustments to prioritize activities that align with God's purposes. Create a schedule that includes time for prayer, Bible study, fellowship, and service. Be intentional about using your time wisely and productively. Surround yourself with wise and godly individuals who can provide guidance and support. Seek advice from mentors, pastors, or mature believers when faced with important decisions. Value their wisdom and experience as you seek to understand God's will.

Be filled with the Spirit: Seek to be continually filled with the Holy Spirit, surrendering to His leading and depending on His power. This involves a daily commitment to walk in the Spirit and to be guided by His presence. Reflect on your relationship with the Holy Spirit. Are there areas where you need to surrender more fully to His leading? Ask God to fill you with His Spirit and to help you live a life that reflects His presence and power.

Start each day with a prayer of surrender, inviting the Holy Spirit to fill and guide you. Acknowledge your dependence on His power and seek His presence in all that you do. Cultivate a habit of listening to the Spirit's promptings and obeying His leading.

Participate actively in corporate worship and fellowship. Join in singing psalms, hymns, and spiritual songs with your church family. Let your worship reflect your joy and gratitude to God, encouraging others to do the same.

Cultivate a life of worship and thanksgiving: Embrace a lifestyle of worship and thanksgiving, expressing your gratitude to God in all circumstances. This involves a heart that is continually focused on God and His goodness. thanksgiving and worship. Are there some ways you can incorporate more expressions of gratitude and praise into your life? Spend time each day giving thanks to God for His blessings and faithfulness.

Keep a journal where you record daily blessings and reasons for gratitude. Reflect on God's faithfulness and goodness in your life, and let this practice cultivate a heart of thanksgiving. Set aside time each day for personal worship. This can include singing, playing an instrument, or simply reflecting on God's attributes and expressing your love for Him. Let worship be a regular part of your routine, not just reserved for Sundays.

Develop the habit of giving thanks in all situations, both good and challenging. Recognize God's sovereignty and trust in His plans, even when circumstances are difficult. Let your attitude of gratitude be a witness to others of your faith and trust in God.

Conclusion

In this passage, Paul challenges us to live as children of light, reflecting the character of Christ in our daily lives. We are called to imitate God's love, to cultivate purity and integrity, to live as light in a dark world, to expose and reject darkness, to walk in wisdom, to be filled with the Spirit, and to cultivate a life of worship and thanksgiving.

As we reflect on this passage, let us be inspired by Paul's exhortation and encouraged by the transformation that God has brought about in our lives.

Let us seek to live in a way that reflects our new identity in Christ, contributing to the growth and health of the body of Christ and may we carry the truths of Ephesians in our hearts and live out our faith boldly and joyfully.

11. HOUSEKEEPING

The Apostle Paul now provides instructions for Christian households. He addresses relationships between husbands and wives, parents and children, and masters and slaves. This passage is really foundational for understanding how we are to live out our faith in our closest relationships, emphasizing mutual submission, love, respect, and integrity.

> **Ephesians 5:21-6:9** *"Submit to one another out of reverence for Christ. Wives, submit yourselves to your own husbands as you do to the Lord. For the husband is the head of the wife as Christ is the head of the church, his body, of which he is the Savior. Now as the church submits to Christ, so also wives should submit to their husbands in everything.*
>
> *Husbands, love your wives, just as Christ loved the church and gave himself up for her to make her holy, cleansing her by the washing with water through the word, and to present her to himself as a radiant church, without stain or wrinkle or any other blemish, but holy and blameless.*
>
> *In this same way, husbands ought to love their wives as their own bodies. He who loves his wife loves himself. After all, no one ever hated their own body, but they feed and care for their body, just as Christ does the church - for we are members of his body.* '
>
> *For this reason, a man will leave his father and mother and be united to his wife, and the two will become one flesh.*' *This is a profound mystery - but I am talking about Christ and the church. However, each one of you also must love his wife as he loves himself, and the wife must respect her husband.*

Children, obey your parents in the Lord, for this is right. 'Honor your father and mother' - which is the first commandment with a promise -'so that it may go well with you and that you may enjoy long life on the earth.' Fathers, do not exasperate your children; instead, bring them up in the training and instruction of the Lord.

Slaves, obey your earthly masters with respect and fear, and with sincerity of heart, just as you would obey Christ. Obey them not only to win their favour when their eye is on you, but as slaves of Christ, doing the will of God from your heart. Serve wholeheartedly, as if you were serving the Lord, not people, because you know that the Lord will reward each one for whatever good they do, whether they are slave or free.

And masters, treat your slaves in the same way. Do not threaten them, since you know that he who is both their Master and yours is in heaven, and there is no favouritism with him."

This passage can be divided into four main sections: the call to mutual submission (5:21), instructions for husbands and wives (5:22-33), instructions for children and parents (6:1-4), and instructions for slaves and masters (6:5-9). Each section provides us with practical guidance on how to live out our faith in our closest relationships, reflecting the love and grace of Christ.

The call to mutual submission (5:21)

Paul begins this passage with a foundational principle: *"Submit to one another out of reverence for Christ."* This call to mutual submission sets the tone for the specific instructions that follow. It emphasizes the importance of humility, respect, and love in all our relationships.

Mutual submission is rooted in our reverence for Christ. As believers, we are called to follow the example of Jesus, who demonstrated the ultimate act of submission by laying down His life for us. Our submission to one another is an expression of our love for Christ and our desire to honour Him in all that we do.

Mutual submission involves a willingness to put others' needs and interests above our own. It requires us to cultivate an attitude of humility and to seek the well-being of others. This principle applies to all our relationships, whether in the home, the church, or the workplace.

Instructions for husbands and wives (5:22-33)

Paul provides specific instructions for husbands and wives, highlighting the importance of love and respect in marriage.

Wives: *"Wives, submit yourselves to your own husbands as you do to the Lord. For the husband is the head of the wife as Christ is the head of the church, his body, of which he is the Savior. Now as the church submits to Christ, so also wives should submit to their husbands in everything."*

Paul calls wives to submit to their husbands as they do to the Lord. This submission is not about inferiority or subjugation but about honouring the God-given order in the family. Just as the church submits to Christ, wives are called to submit to their husbands, recognizing their role as the head of the family.

This submission is voluntary and motivated by love and respect. It reflects a desire to support and honour the husband's leadership, fostering unity and harmony in the marriage.

Husbands: "*Husbands, love your wives, just as Christ loved the church and gave himself up for her to make her holy, cleansing her by the washing with water through the word, and to present her to himself as a radiant church, without stain or wrinkle or any other blemish, but holy and blameless. In this same way, husbands ought to love their wives as their own bodies. He who loves his wife loves himself. After all, no one ever hated their own body, but they feed and care for their body, just as Christ does the church - for we are members of his body.*"

Paul calls husbands to love their wives as Christ loved the church. This love is sacrificial, selfless, and unconditional. Just as Christ gave Himself up for the church, husbands are called to lay down their lives for their wives, seeking their well-being and spiritual growth. Husbands are to love their wives as their own bodies, providing for their needs and caring for them with tenderness and compassion. This love reflects the unity and oneness of marriage, where husband and wife are united as one flesh.

The Profound Mystery: "*For this reason a man will leave his father and mother and be united to his wife, and the two will become one flesh.' This is a profound mystery - but I am talking about Christ and the church. However, each one of you also must love his wife as he loves himself, and the wife must respect her husband.*"

Paul concludes this section by highlighting the profound mystery of marriage, which reflects the relationship between Christ and the church. The union of husband and wife is a picture of the unity and intimacy between Christ and His people. Paul summarizes his instructions with a call for husbands to love their wives and for wives to respect their husbands. Love and respect are essential for a healthy and thriving marriage, reflecting the character of Christ and His love for the church.

Instructions for children and parents (6:1-4)

Paul provides instructions for children and parents, emphasizing the importance of obedience, honour, and nurturing in the family.

Children: "*Children, obey your parents in the Lord, for this is right. 'Honor your father and mother' - which is the first commandment with a promise - so that it may go well with you and that you may enjoy long life on the earth.'*"

Paul calls children to obey their parents in the Lord, recognizing that this is the right and proper thing to do. Obedience to parents is an expression of respect and honour, reflecting the order and authority established by God in the family.

Paul cites the fifth commandment, which comes with a promise of blessing: "*Honour your father and mother so that it may go well with you and that you may enjoy long life on the earth.*" Honouring parents leads to a flourishing and blessed life, reflecting the wisdom and goodness of God's design for the family.

Fathers: "*Fathers, do not exasperate your children; instead, bring them up in the training and instruction of the Lord.*" Paul addresses fathers specifically, calling them to nurture and guide their children without exasperating or provoking them to anger. Fathers are to provide loving discipline and instruction, helping their children grow in the knowledge and fear of the Lord.

This involves creating an strong environment of love, encouragement, and support, where children can thrive and develop into mature and godly individuals.

Fathers are called to always be patient, understanding, and consistent in their parenting, reflecting the character of God the Father.

Instructions for slaves and masters (6:5-9)

Paul provides instructions here for slaves and masters, emphasizing the importance of integrity, respect, and fairness in the workplace. At no point does Paul condone slavery, he merely addresses the reality of his time and talks about the attitude of our hearts, regardless of our situation.

Slaves: "*Slaves, obey your earthly masters with respect and fear, and with sincerity of heart, just as you would obey Christ. Obey them not only to win their favour when their eye is on you, but as slaves of Christ, doing the will of God from your heart. Serve wholeheartedly, as if you were serving the Lord, not people, because you know that the Lord will reward each one for whatever good they do, whether they are slave or free.*"

Paul calls slaves to obey their earthly masters with respect and sincerity, recognizing that their ultimate obedience is to Christ. Slaves are to serve wholeheartedly, as if they were serving the Lord, not people. This attitude transforms their work into an act of worship and service to God.

Paul emphasizes that the Lord will reward each person for the good they do, whether they are slave or free. This assurance of divine reward provides motivation and encouragement for slaves to serve faithfully and diligently, knowing that their labour is not in vain.

Masters: "*And masters, treat your slaves in the same way. Do not threaten them, since you know that he who is both their Master and yours is in heaven, and there is no favouritism with him.*"

Paul addresses masters, calling them to treat their slaves with respect and fairness, recognizing that they too have a Master in heaven. Masters are to avoid threatening or mistreating their slaves, understanding that they are accountable to God for their actions.

This instruction challenges the prevailing cultural norms of the time and calls for a rather radical transformation in the relationship between masters and slaves. It emphasizes the equality and dignity of all people before God, who shows no favouritism.

Practical Applications

Embrace mutual submission: Reflect on the principle of mutual submission and consider how it can be applied in your relationships. Are there areas where you need to demonstrate more humility, respect, and love? Ask God to help you cultivate an attitude of mutual submission, seeking to honour and serve others out of reverence for Christ.

In your marriage, strive to support and honour your spouse, recognizing their unique role and value. In your family, seek to nurture and guide your children with patience and understanding.

In your workplace, treat your colleagues and employees with respect and fairness, recognizing their dignity and worth.

Look for small, everyday opportunities to serve others in your family, church, and community. Whether it's helping with household chores, volunteering at church, or offering assistance to a neighbour, these acts of service reflect an attitude of mutual submission.

Practice active listening in your relationships, seeking to understand and empathize with others. This involves giving your full attention, asking questions, and showing genuine interest and concern. Active listening fosters mutual respect and strengthens relationships.

Approach conflicts with a spirit of humility and a desire for reconciliation. Seek to understand the other person's perspective and to find common ground as you work together to find a resolution that honours God and respects each other.

Foster love and respect in marriage: Husbands, reflect on how you can love your wives as Christ loved the church. Consider ways to demonstrate sacrificial love, seeking the well-being and spiritual growth of your wife. Wives, reflect on how you can respect your husbands, honouring their leadership and supporting them in their role.

Take some time to communicate with your spouse and to understand their needs and desires. Pray together and seek God's guidance in your marriage. Commit to loving and respecting each other, fostering unity and harmony in your relationship. Set aside regular time to spend with your spouse, engaging in activities that strengthen your relationship.

Look for opportunities to affirm and encourage your spouse. Express appreciation for their efforts and qualities and offer encouragement and support. Affirmation and encouragement build trust and strengthen the bond between husband and wife. Pray together and seek to grow spiritually as a couple. Study God's Word together, attend church services and small groups, and support each other in your faith journey. Spiritual growth fosters unity and deepens your relationship with each other and with God.

Cultivate obedience and honour in the family: Children, reflect on how you can obey and honour your parents, recognizing the wisdom and goodness of God's design for the family. Parents, reflect on how you can nurture and guide your children without exasperating them. Seek to create an environment of love, encouragement, and support, helping your children grow in the knowledge and fear of the Lord.

Take time to listen to your children and to understand their needs and concerns. Always provide loving discipline and instruction, helping them develop into mature and godly individuals. Pray for each of your children and seek God's guidance in your parenting.

Establish a regular time for family devotions, where you read the Bible, pray, and discuss spiritual matters together. Family devotions create a foundation of faith and provide opportunities for teaching and discipleship.

Use positive reinforcement to encourage obedience and honour in your children. Praise and reward good behaviour and provide constructive feedback and guidance. Positive reinforcement fosters a sense of accomplishment and motivates children to continue growing in their faith and character.

Model the behaviour you want to see in your children. Demonstrate respect, kindness, and obedience in your own actions and interactions. Children learn by observing their parents, so your example is a powerful tool for teaching and guiding them.

Practice integrity and respect in the workplace: Employees, reflect on how you can serve your employers with respect and sincerity, recognizing that your ultimate obedience is to Christ.

Employers, reflect on how you can treat your employees with respect and fairness, recognizing their dignity and worth. In your work, strive to serve wholeheartedly, as if you were serving the Lord, not people. Recognize the value and importance of your work and seek to honour God in all that you do. Treat your colleagues and employees with kindness and respect, fostering a positive and supportive work environment.

Strive for excellence in your work, doing your best in all tasks and responsibilities. Excellence reflects integrity and respect for your employer and colleagues. It also honours God, who calls us to do our work as unto Him.

Invest in your professional development by seeking opportunities for growth and improvement. Attend workshops, take courses, and seek mentorship to enhance your skills and knowledge. Professional development demonstrates a commitment to integrity and excellence.

Adhere to ethical practices in all aspects of your work. Be honest and transparent in your dealings and avoid actions that compromise your integrity. Ethical practices build trust and respect in the workplace and reflect the character of Christ.

Conclusion

In this passage, Paul provides instructions for Christian households, emphasizing the importance of mutual submission, love, respect, and integrity in our closest relationships. We are called to honour and serve one another out of reverence for Christ, reflecting His love and grace in our interactions with family members, colleagues, and employees.

As we reflect on this passage, let us be inspired by Paul's exhortation and encouraged by the transformation that God has brought about in our lives.

Let us seek to live in a way that reflects our new identity in Christ, contributing to the growth and health of our families, churches, and workplaces.

12. THE ARMOUR OF GOD

We now reach a powerful and crucial passage in our study of the book of Ephesians. Paul exhorts us here to be strong in the Lord and to put on the full armour of God. This passage provides us with essential guidance on how to stand firm against the spiritual forces of evil and to live victoriously in our Christian walk.

> **Ephesians 6:10-20** *"Finally, be strong in the Lord and in his mighty power. Put on the full armour of God, so that you can take your stand against the devil's schemes. For our struggle is not against flesh and blood, but against the rulers, against the authorities, against the powers of this dark world and against the spiritual forces of evil in the heavenly realms.*
>
> *Therefore put on the full armour of God, so that when the day of evil comes, you may be able to stand your ground, and after you have done everything, to stand. Stand firm then, with the belt of truth buckled around your waist, with the breastplate of righteousness in place, and with your feet fitted with the readiness that comes from the gospel of peace.*
>
> *In addition to all this, take up the shield of faith, with which you can extinguish all the flaming arrows of the evil one. Take the helmet of salvation and the sword of the Spirit, which is the word of God. And pray in the Spirit on all occasions with all kinds of prayers and requests. With this in mind, be alert and always keep on praying for all the Lord's people.*
>
> *Pray also for me, that whenever I speak, words may be given me so that I will fearlessly make known the mystery of the gospel, for which I am an ambassador in chains. Pray that I may declare it fearlessly, as I should."*

This passage can be divided into three main sections: the call to be strong in the Lord (verses 10-13), the description of the full armour of God (verses 14-17), and the exhortation to pray in the Spirit (verses 18-20). Each section provides us with practical guidance on how to stand firm in our faith and to live victoriously in the face of spiritual warfare.

The call to be strong in the Lord (6:10-13)

Paul begins this passage with a powerful exhortation: *"Finally, be strong in the Lord and in his mighty power."* This call to be strong is not about relying on our own strength but about drawing our strength from the Lord and His mighty power. The Christian life is a spiritual battle, and we need God's strength to stand firm.

Paul continues, *"Put on the full armour of God, so that you can take your stand against the devil's schemes."* The armour of God is essential for standing against the enemy's attacks. The devil is a cunning adversary who uses various schemes and tactics to deceive and destroy. We must be vigilant and prepared for battle.

Paul emphasizes that our struggle is not against flesh and blood but against spiritual forces: *"For our struggle is not against flesh and blood, but against the rulers, against the authorities, against the powers of this dark world and against the spiritual forces of evil in the heavenly realms."* This reminder shifts our focus from earthly conflicts to the spiritual battle that lies behind them.

The spiritual forces of evil are powerful and organized, operating in the heavenly realms. They seek to oppose God's work and to hinder our faith. Recognizing the true nature of our battle helps us to understand the importance of spiritual armour and the need for divine strength.

Paul reiterates the importance of the full armour of God: *"Therefore put on the full armour of God, so that when the day of evil comes, you may be able to stand your ground, and after you have done everything, to stand."* The day of evil refers to times of intense spiritual attack and temptation. In these moments, we need to be fully equipped and ready to stand firm.

The description of the full armour of God (6:14-17)

Paul provides a detailed description of the full armour of God, using the imagery of a Roman soldier's armour to illustrate the spiritual resources available to us. Even though this is a great illustration Paul uses, and one which would have been very clear to original readers or hearers, **we need to be very careful we do not misinterpret this analogy.**

All too often I hear people emphasising the two words, *"put on"* and by inference, they imply that believers do not have this armour unless they put it on through prayer or some ritualistic process. This is a complete misunderstanding of our reality in Christ and it sets a very dangerous precedent for what is often akin to witchcraft.

When we unpack each of these 'pieces' of armour, we will realise that all of them are characteristics of Jesus Christ. Truth, righteousness, peace, faith etc. are all gifted to us in Christ and as believers, Christ is already in us. We never wake up one morning without Christ within us.

So, we never wake up without our armour on. Millions of people 'put on' the armour of God in prayer each morning and when they forget to, they attribute anything bad that happens that day to their neglect in putting on the armour of God. This is absolute nonsense and complete heresy.

You <u>have</u> the armour of God by virtue of the gift of Jesus Christ. You don't have to 'put on' Jesus every day and nor are you without Jesus if you forget to put Him on. So too with the armour of God. I really wish the Greek in this passage would have been translated differently so as to avoid this confusion.

To be consistent with the truth of who we are in Christ, it would be better to say, *"Remember you have the armour of God ..."* or *"Stand firm in the armour of God."* When we say, *"Put on the armour of God"* it makes it sound like we didn't have it before we made a conscious choice to put it on. The fact that some people do this every day, makes it even more ridiculous. If you put on the armour of God yesterday, why are you putting it on again today? When did you take it off? Did it fall off? Did you lose it in battle? Pretty poor armour if it doesn't even stay on!

The fact is this: **God put His armour on you when He redeemed you in Christ and filled you to the measure with all the fullness of Christ.** It is an affront to God Himself for you to even suggest you have to put on something which only God can put on you!

Therefore, in all our discussion of this illustration, always understand that when we talk about "putting on" the armour of God, we are actually talking about embracing, using, applying or standing in the armour of God which is already ours in Christ. So, let's work through the various aspects of the armour which has been given to us on Christ.

The belt of truth ...

"Stand firm then, with the belt of truth buckled around your waist." The belt of truth represents the foundational role of truth in the Christian life.

Truth holds everything together, providing stability and integrity. It involves a commitment to God's truth and a rejection of falsehood and deception.

Truth is essential for standing firm against the enemy's lies. It involves knowing and living by the truth of God's Word, allowing it to shape our thoughts, attitudes, and actions. The belt of truth empowers us to discern and reject the enemy's schemes.

The breastplate of righteousness ...

"With the breastplate of righteousness in place." The breastplate protects the vital organs, particularly the heart. The breastplate of righteousness represents the righteousness that comes from God through faith in Christ. It involves living a life of integrity and moral uprightness.

Righteousness protects us from the enemy's attacks on our character and conduct. It involves pursuing holiness and living in accordance with God's standards. The breastplate of righteousness empowers us to resist temptation and to stand firm in our faith.

The shoes of the gospel of peace ...

"And with your feet fitted with the readiness that comes from the gospel of peace." The shoes enable a soldier to stand firm and to move swiftly. The shoes of the gospel of peace represent the readiness and stability that come from the good news of Jesus Christ.

The gospel of peace provides a firm foundation for our lives. It involves being grounded in the message of salvation and being ready to share it with others. The shoes of the gospel of peace empower us to stand firm in our faith and to advance God's kingdom.

The shield of faith ...

"In addition to all this, take up the shield of faith, with which you can extinguish all the flaming arrows of the evil one." The shield provides protection from the enemy's attacks. The shield of faith represents our trust and confidence in God and His promises.

Faith is essential for deflecting the enemy's flaming arrows: doubts, fears, temptations, and accusations. It involves trusting in God's character, promises, and power. The shield of faith empowers us to stand firm and to resist the enemy's attacks.

The helmet of salvation ...

"Take the helmet of salvation." The helmet protects the head, the seat of the mind. The helmet of salvation represents the assurance and security that come from knowing we are saved by God's grace through faith in Christ. Salvation guards our minds from the enemy's attacks on our identity and security. It involves having a confident assurance of our salvation and living in the reality of God's saving grace. The helmet of salvation empowers us to stand firm in our identity as children of God.

The sword of the Spirit ...

"And the sword of the Spirit, which is the word of God." The sword is both an offensive and defensive weapon. The sword of the Spirit represents the Word of God, which is powerful and effective for spiritual battle. The Word of God is essential for countering the enemy's lies and for standing firm in the truth. It involves knowing, meditating on, and applying God's Word in our lives. The sword of the Spirit empowers us to stand firm and to advance God's kingdom.

The exhortation to pray in the Spirit (6:18-20)

Paul concludes this passage with an exhortation to pray in the Spirit: "*And pray in the Spirit on all occasions with all kinds of prayers and requests. With this in mind, be alert and always keep on praying for all the Lord's people.*"

Prayer is an essential part of spiritual warfare. It involves constant communication with God, seeking His guidance, strength, and protection. Praying in the Spirit means praying in alignment with God's will and being led by the Holy Spirit. Paul emphasizes the importance of being alert and persistent in prayer. We are called to pray on all occasions, with all kinds of prayers and requests. This involves being watchful and vigilant, recognizing the ongoing spiritual battle and the need for God's intervention.

Paul also asks for prayer for himself: "*Pray also for me, that whenever I speak, words may be given me so that I will fearlessly make known the mystery of the gospel, for which I am an ambassador in chains. Pray that I may declare it fearlessly, as I should.*"

Paul's request for prayer highlights the importance of supporting one another in prayer. He recognizes his need for God's strength and guidance in proclaiming the gospel. This reminder encourages us to pray for our leaders, missionaries, and fellow believers, that they may stand firm and boldly proclaim the gospel.

Practical Applications

Be strong in the Lord ...

Reflect on the source of your strength and seek to draw your strength from the Lord and His mighty power.

Recognize that the Christian life is a spiritual battle and that you need God's strength to stand firm. Take time to cultivate your relationship with God through prayer, worship, and the study of His Word. Seek His guidance, strength, and protection in all areas of your life. Establish a regular time for daily devotions, where you read the Bible, pray, and meditate on God's Word. Daily devotions help you draw strength from the Lord and His mighty power.

Engage in regular worship, both privately and corporately. Worship helps you focus on God's greatness and power, reminding you of His strength and majesty. Incorporate prayer and fasting into your spiritual disciplines. Prayer and fasting help you seek God's guidance and strength, deepening your reliance on Him.

Put on the full armour of God ...

Make it a daily practice to put on the full armour of God. Reflect on each piece of armour and consider how it applies to your life. Ask God to equip you with His righteousness, truth, peace, faith, salvation, and His Word. Take time to meditate on key Scriptures that remind you of the armour of God. Use these Scriptures in your prayers, asking God to help you stand firm against the enemy's attacks.

Stand firm in Truth ...

Commit to knowing and living by the truth of God's Word. Reject falsehood and deception and seek to live a life of integrity and honesty. Truth is essential for standing firm against the enemy's lies.

Take time to study and meditate on God's Word daily. Allow His truth to shape your thoughts, attitudes, and actions. Seek to apply His truth in all areas of your life.

Join a Bible study group to deepen your understanding of God's Word. Bible study helps you know and live by the truth, providing a solid foundation for your faith. Practice honesty and integrity in your relationships. Seek to live a life of truth and transparency, reflecting God's truth in your interactions with others. Be discerning in your consumption of media. Choose content that aligns with God's truth and avoid content that promotes falsehood and deception.

Pursue righteousness ...

Commit to living a life of righteousness and moral uprightness. Pursue holiness and seek to live in accordance with God's standards. Righteousness protects you from the enemy's attacks on your character and conduct. Reflect on areas of your life where you need to pursue greater righteousness. Ask God to help you grow in holiness and to live a life that honours Him.

Be grounded in the gospel of peace ...

Reflect on the message of the gospel and seek to be grounded in its truth. Allow the gospel to provide stability and readiness in your life. Be ready to share the good news of Jesus Christ with others. Take time to reflect on the significance of the gospel in your life. Ask God to help you live in the reality of His peace and to be ready to share the gospel with others.

Strengthen your faith ...

Cultivate a strong and unwavering faith in God and His promises. Trust in His character, promises, and power. Faith is essential for deflecting the enemy's flaming arrows of doubt, fear, and temptation.

Reflect on areas where you need to strengthen your faith. Take time to pray and ask God to help you trust Him more fully. Seek to grow in your knowledge of His character and promises.

Guard your mind with the helmet of salvation ...

Reflect on the assurance and security that come from knowing you are saved by God's grace through faith in Christ. Guard your mind from the enemy's attacks on your identity and security.

Take time to reflect on the significance of your salvation. Ask God to help you live in the reality of His saving grace and to guard your mind from doubts and fears.

Wield the sword of the Spirit ...

Commit to knowing, meditating on, and applying God's Word in your life. The Word of God is powerful and effective for spiritual battle. Use it to counter the enemy's lies and to stand firm in the truth. Take time to memorize and meditate on key Scriptures that remind you of God's truth and promises. Use these Scriptures in your prayers and in your daily life.

Pray in the Spirit ...

Make prayer a central part of your spiritual life. Pray on all occasions, with all kinds of prayers and requests. Be alert and persistent in prayer, recognizing the ongoing spiritual battle and the need for God's intervention. Take time to develop a habit of prayer. Set aside regular times for prayer and seek to pray continually throughout your day. Ask the Holy Spirit to guide your prayers and to help you pray in alignment with God's will.

Conclusion

In this passage, Paul exhorts us to be strong in the Lord and to put on the full armour of God, emphasizing the importance of standing firm against the spiritual forces of evil. We are called to draw our strength from the Lord and His mighty power, to put on the full armour of God, and to pray in the Spirit on all occasions.

As we reflect on this passage, let us be inspired by Paul's exhortation and encouraged by the resources that God has provided for us. Let us seek to live in a way that reflects our new identity in Christ, standing firm in our faith and living victoriously in the face of spiritual warfare.

13. FINAL EXHORTATIONS

We come now to the end of our journey through the book of Ephesians with the Apostle Paul's final exhortations. In these closing few verses, Paul offers personal remarks, shares news about his circumstances, and gives a final blessing. Though these verses are brief, they are rich with encouragement, community, and grace, offering us profound insights into living out our faith and staying connected as the body of Christ.

> **Ephesians 6:21-24** *"Tychicus, the dear brother and faithful servant in the Lord, will tell you everything, so that you also may know how I am and what I am doing. I am sending him to you for this very purpose, that you may know how we are, and that he may encourage you. Peace to the brothers and sisters, and love with faith from God the Father and the Lord Jesus Christ. Grace to all who love our Lord Jesus Christ with an undying love."*

This passage can be divided into three main sections: Paul's commendation of Tychicus (21-22), his final blessing to the Ephesians (23-24), and reflections on the overall message of Ephesians. Each section provides us with practical guidance on living out our faith, staying connected in community, and embracing the grace and love of God.

Paul's commendation of Tychicus (6:21-22)

Paul begins by introducing Tychicus, a dear brother and faithful servant in the Lord: *"Tychicus, the dear brother and faithful servant in the Lord, will tell you everything, so that you also may know how I am and what I am doing. I am sending him to you for this very purpose, that you may know how we are, and that he may encourage you."*

Tychicus is mentioned several times in the New Testament as a trusted companion and co-worker of Paul. Here, Paul highlights Tychicus's role in conveying news about Paul's circumstances and providing some encouragement to the Ephesian believers.

Tychicus's character ...

Paul describes Tychicus as a dear brother and a faithful servant in the Lord. This commendation serves to highlight Tychicus's character and dedication to the ministry. He is a beloved member of the Christian community and a most trustworthy messenger.

The term "dear brother" emphasizes the close relationship between Paul and Tychicus. This language reflects the deep bonds of fellowship and love that characterize the Christian community. It reminds us of the importance of building and maintaining strong, supportive relationships within the body of Christ.

The description *"faithful servant in the Lord"* underscores Tychicus's reliability and commitment to serving Christ. Faithfulness is a key attribute in Christian service, and Tychicus exemplifies this quality through his dedication to supporting Paul and the early church.

Tychicus's mission ...

Paul states that he is sending Tychicus to the Ephesians so that they may know how Paul and his companions are doing and that Tychicus may encourage them. This mission involves both communication and encouragement. Communication is essential for maintaining connection and unity within the church.

By sending Tychicus with news about his circumstances, Paul ensures that the Ephesians are informed and reassured about his well-being. This transparency fosters trust and solidarity within the Christian community.

Encouragement is another crucial aspect of Tychicus's mission. Paul recognizes the importance of uplifting and strengthening the believers, especially in times of trial and uncertainty. Tychicus's presence and words are meant to provide comfort and motivation, helping the Ephesians remain steadfast in their faith.

Paul's final blessing to the Ephesians (6:23-24)

Paul concludes his letter with a final blessing, invoking peace, love, faith, and grace upon the Ephesian believers: "Peace to the brothers and sisters, and love with faith from God the Father and the Lord Jesus Christ. Grace to all who love our Lord Jesus Christ with an undying love."

Peace ...

Paul begins his blessing with a prayer for peace: "*Peace to the brothers and sisters.*" Peace is a central theme in Paul's letters and a key aspect of the Christian life. It refers to both inner tranquillity and harmonious relationships within the community. The source of true peace is God Himself. Paul emphasizes that this peace comes from "*God the Father and the Lord Jesus Christ.*" It is a divine gift that surpasses human understanding and is rooted in our reconciliation with God through Christ. In a world filled with conflict and turmoil, the peace of God provides stability and assurance. As believers, we are called to be peacemakers, promoting reconciliation and harmony in our relationships. Paul's blessing reminds us to seek and cultivate this peace in our lives and within the church.

Love with faith ...

Paul continues by praying for *"love with faith from God the Father and the Lord Jesus Christ."* Love and faith are foundational to the Christian life, and Paul often pairs these virtues in his letters.

Love is the hallmark of the Christian community. It reflects the selfless, sacrificial love of Christ and is expressed through our actions, attitudes, and relationships. Love binds us together as the body of Christ and is a powerful witness to the world.

Faith in this context is our trust and confidence in God. It involves believing in His promises, relying on His strength, and living in obedience to His Word. Faith sustains us through trials and challenges, enabling us to stand firm in our relationship with God.

Paul emphasizes that both love and faith are gifts from God the Father and the Lord Jesus Christ. They are not qualities we produce on our own but are cultivated through our relationship with God. As we grow in our love for God and our faith in Him, we are empowered to love others and to live out our faith with integrity and purpose.

Grace ...

Paul concludes his blessing with a prayer for grace: "Grace to all who love our Lord Jesus Christ with an undying love." Grace is a central theme in Paul's theology, representing God's unmerited favour and empowerment for the Christian life. Grace is the foundation of our salvation. It is by grace that we are saved through faith, and it is by grace that we are sustained and empowered to live out our faith.

Paul's prayer for grace encompasses both the initial experience of salvation and the ongoing work of God's grace in our lives.

Paul specifically addresses this blessing to "*all who love our Lord Jesus Christ with an undying love.*" This phrase highlights the depth and endurance of our love for Christ. An undying love is steadfast, unwavering, and eternal, reflecting the depth of our commitment to Jesus.

As recipients of God's grace, we are called to extend grace to others. This involves showing kindness, forgiveness, and generosity in our relationships. Paul's blessing reminds us of the abundant grace we have received and encourages us to live in a way that reflects this grace to the world.

Reflections on the overall message of Ephesians

As we conclude our journey through the book of Ephesians, it is important to reflect on the overall message and themes of this powerful letter. Paul's letter to the Ephesians addresses key aspects of Christian doctrine and practice, providing rich insights into our identity in Christ, the unity of the church, and the conduct of believers.

Our identity in Christ ...

One of the central themes of Ephesians is our identity in Christ. Paul emphasizes that we are chosen, redeemed, and sealed by the Holy Spirit. We have been adopted as God's children, and we are heirs of His promises. Our identity in Christ shapes how we live and relate to others. It provides us with a sense of purpose and belonging, empowering us to live in a way that reflects the character of Christ. As we embrace our identity in Christ, we are called to live out the values and virtues of the kingdom of God.

The unity of the Church ...

Another key theme in Ephesians is the unity of the church. Paul emphasizes that the church is the body of Christ, composed of diverse members who are united by their common faith in Jesus. This unity is a reflection of God's eternal plan to bring all things together under Christ.

Paul calls us to maintain the unity of the Spirit through the bond of peace. This involves cultivating humility, gentleness, patience, and love in our relationships. Unity is not uniformity but a harmonious diversity that reflects the richness of God's grace.

The unity of the church is also a powerful witness to the world. As we live out our unity in Christ, we demonstrate the transformative power of the gospel and the reconciling work of God. Paul's vision for the church challenges us to pursue unity and to be a visible expression of God's kingdom on earth.

The conduct of believers ...

Ephesians also provides practical guidance on the conduct of believers. Paul addresses various aspects of Christian living, including our relationships in the home, in the workplace, and in the church. He calls us to live in a way that reflects our new identity in Christ and our commitment to God's standards.

This involves putting off the old self and putting on the new self, living in righteousness and holiness. Paul emphasizes the importance of truth, love, forgiveness, and integrity in our interactions with others. He also addresses the spiritual battle we face and the need to put on the full armour of God.

Paul's instructions are not merely moral guidelines but are rooted in the transformative power of the gospel. As we live out our faith, we are empowered by the Holy Spirit to reflect the character of Christ and to fulfill God's purposes in our lives.

Practical Applications

As we reflect on the message of Ephesians, it is essential to consider how we can practically apply these teachings in our daily lives. The themes of identity, unity, and conduct provide a framework for living out our faith in a way that honours God and builds up the body of Christ.

Embrace and celebrate your identity in Christ ...

> *Daily reminders of your identity:* Remind yourself each day of your identity in Christ. Reflect on key Scriptures that affirm who you are in Him, such as Ephesians 1:3-14, which highlights that you are chosen, redeemed, and sealed by the Holy Spirit. Allow these truths to shape your thoughts and actions throughout the day.
>
> *Live with purpose:* Recognize that your identity in Christ gives you a unique purpose and calling. Seek to discover and fulfill the specific role God has for you within His kingdom. Whether it is through your work, relationships, or ministry, strive to live out your purpose with passion and dedication.
>
> *Find your security in Christ:* In a world that often defines worth and identity by external factors, find your security in Christ alone.
>
> Let go of the need for approval from others and rest in the assurance that you are deeply loved and valued by God.

Pursue and foster unity in the Church ...

> *Cultivate humility and gentleness:* Reflect on Paul's clear exhortation in Ephesians 4:2 to *"be completely humble and gentle; be patient, bearing with one another in love."* Seek to develop these qualities in your interactions with others, recognizing that humility and gentleness are essential for maintaining unity.
>
> *Practice active listening:* Foster unity by actively listening to others, especially those with different perspectives or experiences. Seek to understand their viewpoints and to empathize with their struggles. Active listening promotes mutual respect and understanding within the body of Christ.
>
> *Engage in reconciliation:* When conflicts arise, take the initiative to seek reconciliation. Follow the principles outlined in Matthew 18:15-17 for addressing conflicts in a healthy and constructive manner. Be willing to apologize, forgive, and work towards restoration, prioritizing the unity of the church.

Live out your faith with integrity and love ...

> *Commit to righteous living:* Reflect on Ephesians 4:22-24, which calls us to put off the old self and to put on the new self, created to be like God in true righteousness and holiness. Strive to live a life that reflects the character of Christ, seeking to honour Him in all areas of your life.
>
> *Extend forgiveness:* Embrace Paul's clear exhortation in Ephesians 4:32 to *"be kind and compassionate to one another, forgiving each other, just as in Christ God forgave you."* Let go of grudges and bitterness and then choose to extend forgiveness to those who have wronged you.

Walk in Love: Follow Paul's call in Ephesians 5:1-2 to *"follow God's example, therefore, as dearly loved children and walk in the way of love, just as Christ loved us and gave himself up for us as a fragrant offering and sacrifice to God."* Seek to demonstrate Christ-like love in your relationships, actions, and attitudes.

Equip yourself for spiritual battle:

Put on the full armour of God: Reflect on Ephesians 6:10-18, where Paul describes the full armour of God. Make it a daily practice to put on each piece of armour through prayer, asking God to equip you with His truth, righteousness, peace, faith, salvation, and Word.

Stay vigilant and prayerful: Embrace Paul's exhortation in Ephesians 6:18 to *"pray in the Spirit on all occasions with all kinds of prayers and requests."* Stay vigilant and alert in prayer, seeking God's guidance, strength, and protection in the face of spiritual warfare.

Support and Encourage Others: Recognize the importance of community in spiritual battle. Support and encourage your fellow believers, just as Tychicus was sent to encourage the Ephesians. Pray for one another, share your struggles, and stand together in faith.

Encouragement for the journey ahead

As we conclude our journey through the book of Ephesians, it is important to recognize that the teachings and exhortations Paul provides are not just for the early church but are also relevant for us today. The themes of identity, unity, and conduct are timeless principles that guide us in our walk with Christ.

Embrace the journey ...

Recognize that the Christian life is a journey of growth and transformation. There will be challenges and trials along the way, but God's grace and strength are sufficient for every step. Embrace the journey with faith, knowing that God is with you and will guide you.

Stay connected ...

Stay connected to the body of Christ through fellowship, worship, and service. The church is a source of support, encouragement, and accountability. Engage actively in your church community, building relationships that strengthen your faith and help you grow.

Seek God's presence ...

Prioritize your relationship with God above all else. Spend time in prayer, worship, and the study of His Word. Seek His presence daily, allowing Him to fill you with His peace, love, and grace.

Live out your faith ...

Let the truths of Ephesians shape your daily life. Live out your faith with integrity, love, and purpose. Seek to honour God in all that you do, reflecting His character and fulfilling His calling for your life.

Conclusion

In this passage, Paul offers his closing words and final exhortations to the Ephesian believers, highlighting the importance of strong relationships, peace, love, faith, and grace. As we conclude our journey through the book of Ephesians, let us reflect on the rich insights and practical guidance that Paul has provided.

We are called to embrace our identity in Christ, to maintain the unity of the church, and to live out our faith with integrity and purpose. As we live in community, seek peace, demonstrate love and faith, and extend grace, we reflect the character of Christ and fulfill God's purposes in our lives.

Thank you for joining me on this journey through the book of Ephesians. As we move on from this study, it is my prayer that we may carry the truths of this powerful letter in our hearts and live out our faith boldly and joyfully.

www.ingramcontent.com/pod-product-compliance
Lightning Source LLC
Chambersburg PA
CBHW070030040426
42333CB00040B/1420